"DISCARD"

THE ENCYCLOPEDIA OF PSYCHOACTIVE DRUGS

SERIES 1

SERIES 2

DRUGS
THROUGH
THE AGES

GENERAL EDITOR
Professor Solomon H. Snyder, M.D.

*Distinguished Service Professor of
Neuroscience, Pharmacology, and Psychiatry at
The Johns Hopkins University School of Medicine*

•

ASSOCIATE EDITOR
Professor Barry L. Jacobs, Ph.D.

*Program in Neuroscience, Department of Psychology,
Princeton University*

•

SENIOR EDITORIAL CONSULTANT
Joann Rodgers

*Deputy Director, Office of Public Affairs at
The Johns Hopkins Medical Institutions*

SOLOMON H. SNYDER, M.D. • GENERAL EDITOR

THE ENCYCLOPEDIA OF PSYCHOACTIVE DRUGS

SERIES 2

DRUGS THROUGH THE AGES

JEAN McBEE KNOX

1987
CHELSEA HOUSE PUBLISHERS
NEW YORK • NEW HAVEN • PHILADELPHIA

EDITORIAL DIRECTOR: Nancy Toff
MANAGING EDITOR: Karyn Gullen Browne
COPY CHIEF: Perry Scott King
ART DIRECTOR: Giannella Garrett
ASSISTANT ART DIRECTOR: Carol McDougall
PICTURE EDITOR: Elizabeth Terhune

Staff for DRUGS THROUGH THE AGES:

SENIOR EDITOR: Jane Larkin Crain
ASSOCIATE EDITOR: Paula Edelson
ASSISTANT DESIGNER: Victoria Tomaselli
COPY EDITORS: Sean Dolan, Kathleen McDermott
CAPTIONS: Louise Bloomfield
PICTURE RESEARCH: Mary Leverty
PRODUCTION COORDINATOR: Alma Rodriguez
PRODUCTION ASSISTANT: Karen Dreste

CREATIVE DIRECTOR: Harold Steinberg

COVER: Dali, Salvador. *The Persistence of Memory.* 1931. Oil on canvas,
    9½ x 13". Collection, The Museum of Modern Art, New York. Given anon-
    ymously. Photograph © 1986 The Museum of Modern Art, New York.

Library of Congress Cataloging-in-Publication Data
Knox, Jean.
    Psychoactive drugs through the ages.
    (Encyclopedia of psychoactive drugs. Series 2)
    Includes bibliographies and index.
    1. Psychotropic drugs—History—Juvenile literature. 2. Substance abuse—
History—Juvenile literature. I. Title. II. Series. [DNLM: 1. Psychotropic Drugs—
history. 2. Substance Abuse—history. WM 11.1 K74p]
RM315.K59   1987   615'.788'09   86-26885

ISBN 1-55546-221-9

CONTENTS

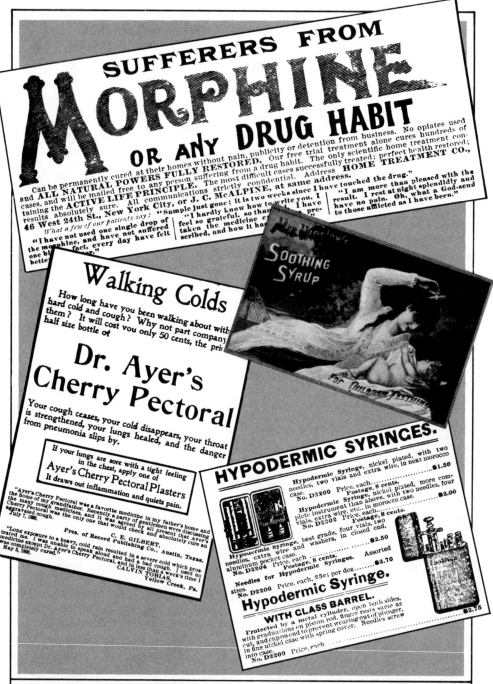

Many drugs hailed as healers in one century have been discovered to be addictive in another. A prime example is the narcotic morphine, which was an ingredient in many 19th-century medications.

In the Mainstream
of American Life

One of the legacies of the social upheaval of the 1960s is that psychoactive drugs have become part of the mainstream of American life. Schools, homes, and communities cannot be "drug proofed." There is a demand for drugs — and the supply is plentiful. Social norms have changed and drugs are not only available—they are everywhere.

But where efforts to curtail the supply of drugs and outlaw their use have had tragically limited effects on demand, it may be that education has begun to stem the rising tide of drug abuse among young people and adults alike.

Over the past 25 years, as drugs have become an increasingly routine facet of contemporary life, a great many teenagers have adopted the notion that drug taking was somehow a right or a privilege or a necessity. They have done so, however, without understanding the consequences of drug use during the crucial years of adolescence.

The teenage years are few in the total life cycle, but critical in the maturation process. During these years adolescents face the difficult tasks of discovering their identity, clarifying their sexual roles, asserting their independence, learning to cope with authority, and searching for goals that will give their lives meaning.

Drugs rob adolescents of precious time, stamina, and health. They interrupt critical learning processes, sometimes forever. Teenagers who use drugs are likely to withdraw increasingly into themselves, to "cop out" at just the time when they most need to reach out and experience the world.

Richard Pryor, shown here in the 1982 film Live on Sunset Strip, *almost lost his life because of drug abuse. He attempted to inhale fumes from cocaine that he was freebasing, a dangerous process that requires heating a highly flammable solution.*

Fortunately, as a recent Gallup poll shows, young people are beginning to realize this, too. They themselves label drugs their most important problem. In the last few years, moreover, the climate of tolerance and ignorance surrounding drugs has been changing.

Adolescents as well as adults are becoming aware of mounting evidence that every race, ethnic group, and class is vulnerable to drug dependency.

Recent publicity about the cost and failure of drug rehabilitation efforts; dangerous drug use among pilots, air traffic controllers, star athletes, and Hollywood celebrities; and drug-related accidents, suicides, and violent crime have focused the public's attention on the need to wage an all-out war on drug abuse before it seriously undermines the fabric of society itself.

The anti-drug message is getting stronger and there is evidence that the message is beginning to get through to adults and teenagers alike.

The Encyclopedia of Psychoactive Drugs hopes to play a part in the national campaign now underway to educate young people about drugs. Series 1 provides clear and comprehensive discussions of common psychoactive substances, outlines their psychological and physiological effects on the mind and body, explains how they "hook" the user, and separates fact from myth in the complex issue of drug abuse.

Whereas Series 1 focuses on specific drugs, such as nicotine or cocaine, Series 2 confronts a broad range of both social and physiological phenomena. Each volume addresses the ramifications of drug use and abuse on some aspect of human experience: social, familial, cultural, historical, and physical. Separate volumes explore questions about the effects of drugs on brain chemistry and unborn children; the use and abuse of painkillers; the relationship between drugs and sexual behavior, sports, and the arts; drugs and disease; the role of drugs in history and the sophisticated drugs now being developed in the laboratory that will profoundly change the future.

Each book in the series is fully illustrated and is tailored to the needs and interests of young readers. The more adolescents know about drugs and their role in society, the less likely they are to misuse them.

Joann Rodgers
Senior Editorial Consultant

This 13th-century Mesopotamian manuscript shows a doctor preparing a medication. Opium, a popular medicine in the ancient and medieval Near East, was first used there around 4000 B.C.E. It has been used as a pain reliever for millenia and still has an important role in modern medicine. Morphine is just one of the drugs derived from opium.

INTRODUCTION

The Gift of Wizardry
Use and Abuse

JACK H. MENDELSON, M.D.
NANCY K. MELLO, PH.D.
Alcohol and Drug Abuse Research Center
Harvard Medical School—McLean Hospital

Dorothy to the Wizard:

"I think you are a very bad man," said Dorothy.
"Oh no, my dear; I'm really a very good man; but I'm a very bad Wizard."

—from THE WIZARD OF OZ

Man is endowed with the gift of wizardry, a talent for discovery and invention. The discovery and invention of substances that change the way we feel and behave are among man's special accomplishments, and, like so many other products of our wizardry, these substances have the capacity to harm as well as to help. Psychoactive drugs can cause profound changes in the chemistry of the brain and other vital organs, and although their legitimate use can relieve pain and cure disease, their abuse leads in a tragic number of cases to destruction.

Consider alcohol — available to all and yet regarded with intense ambivalence from biblical times to the present day. The use of alcoholic beverages dates back to our earliest ancestors. Alcohol use and misuse became associated with the worship of gods and demons. One of the most powerful Greek gods was Dionysus, lord of fruitfulness and god of wine. The Romans adopted Dionysus but changed his name to Bacchus. Festivals and holidays associated with Bacchus celebrated the harvest and the origins of life. Time has blurred the images of the Bacchanalian festival, but the theme of drunkenness as a major part of celebration has survived the pagan gods and remains a familiar part of modern society. The term "Bacchanalian Festival" conveys a more appealing image than "drunken orgy" or "pot party," but whatever the label, drinking alcohol is a form of drug use that results in addiction for millions.

The fact that many millions of other people can use alcohol in moderation does not mitigate the toll this drug takes on society as a whole. According to reliable estimates, one out of every ten Americans develops a serious alcohol-related problem sometime in his or her lifetime. In addition, automobile accidents caused by drunken drivers claim the lives of tens of thousands every year. Many of the victims are gifted young people, just starting out in adult life. Hospital emergency rooms abound with patients seeking help for alcohol-related injuries.

Who is to blame? Can we blame the many manufacturers who produce such an amazing variety of alcoholic beverages? Should we blame the educators who fail to explain the perils of intoxication, or so exaggerate the dangers of drinking that no one could possibly believe them? Are friends to blame — those peers who urge others to "drink more and faster," or the macho types who stress the importance of being able to "hold your liquor"? Casting blame, however, is hardly constructive, and pointing the finger is a fruitless way to deal with the problem. Alcoholism and drug abuse have few culprits but many victims. Accountability begins with each of us, every time we choose to use or misuse an intoxicating substance.

It is ironic that some of man's earliest medicines, derived from natural plant products, are used today to poison and to intoxicate. Relief from pain and suffering is one of society's many continuing goals. Over 3,000 years ago, the Therapeutic Papyrus of Thebes, one of our earliest written records, gave instructions for the use of opium in the treatment of pain. Opium, in the form of its major derivative, morphine, and similar compounds, such as heroin, have also been used by many to induce changes in mood and feeling. Another example of man's misuse of a natural substance is the coca leaf, which for centuries was used by the Indians of Peru to reduce fatigue and hunger. Its modern derivative, cocaine, has important medical use as a local anesthetic. Unfortunately, its increasing abuse in the 1980s clearly has reached epidemic proportions.

The purpose of this series is to explore in depth the psychological and behavioral effects that psychoactive drugs have on the individual, and also, to investigate the ways in which drug use influences the legal, economic, cultural, and even moral aspects of societies. The information presented here (and in other books in this series) is based on many clinical and laboratory studies and other observations by people from diverse walks of life.

Over the centuries, novelists, poets, and dramatists have provided us with many insights into the sometimes seductive but ultimately problematic aspects of alcohol and drug use. Physicians, lawyers, biologists, psychologists, and social scientists have contributed to a better understanding of the causes and consequences of using these substances. The authors in this series have attempted to gather and condense all the latest information about drug use and abuse. They have also described the sometimes wide gaps in our knowledge and have suggested some new ways to answer many difficult questions.

One such question, for example, is how do alcohol and drug problems get started? And what is the best way to treat them when they do? Not too many years ago, alcoholics and drug abusers were regarded as evil, immoral, or both. It is now recognized that these persons suffer from very complicated diseases involving deep psychological and social problems. To understand how the disease begins and progresses, it is necessary to understand the nature of the substance, the behavior of addicts, and the characteristics of the society or culture in which they live.

Although many of the social environments we live in are very similar, some of the most subtle differences can strongly influence our thinking and behavior. Where we live, go to school and work, whom we discuss things with — all influence our opinions about drug use and misuse. Yet we also share certain commonly accepted beliefs that outweigh any differences in our attitudes. The authors in this series have tried to identify and discuss the central, most crucial issues concerning drug use and misuse.

Despite the increasing sophistication of the chemical substances we create in the laboratory, we have a long way to go in our efforts to make these powerful drugs work for us rather than against us.

The volumes in this series address a wide range of timely questions. What influence has drug use had on the arts? Why do so many of today's celebrities and star athletes use drugs, and what is being done to solve this problem? What is the relationship between drugs and crime? What is the physiological basis for the power drugs can hold over us? These are but a few of the issues explored in this far-ranging series.

Educating people about the dangers of drugs can go a long way towards minimizing the desperate consequences of substance abuse for individuals and society as a whole. Luckily, human beings have the resources to solve even the most serious problems that beset them, once they make the commitment to do so. As one keen and sensitive observer, Dr. Lewis Thomas, has said,

> There is nothing at all absurd about the human condition. We matter. It seems to me a good guess, hazarded by a good many people who have thought about it, that we may be engaged in the formation of something like a mind for the life of this planet. If this is so, we are still at the most primitive stage, still fumbling with language and thinking, but infinitely capacitated for the future. Looked at this way, it is remarkable that we've come as far as we have in so short a period, really no time at all as geologists measure time. We are the newest, youngest, and the brightest thing around.

A Greek wine vessel, decorated to represent a woman's face. Alcohol was a religious, medical, and dietary fixture in ancient Greece, and many elaborate rituals were attached to its consumption.

AUTHOR'S PREFACE

It is not difficult to imagine how our prehistoric ancestors might have first stumbled upon mind-altering substances. A group of primitive hunters foraging for food might have sampled some unusual mushrooms, and returned delirious to their campfire. A forgotten jar of ripe fruit may have fermented, and just before the disappointing mash was tossed out, some thirsty cave dweller might have devoured it. Of course, we can only guess when these accidental discoveries were made. What we do know for sure is that the history of drug use is nearly as old as the history of humankind.

Anthropologists offer different dates and locations for the first regular use of psychoactive substances. Alcohol is the drug for which we have some of the earliest archeological evidence. Simple clay beakers, or wide-mouthed drinking cups, dating from about 7000 B.C.E. (B.C.E., Before Common Era, is equivalent to B.C.) have been found in Anatolia, in what is now the country of Turkey. They probably held a yeasty, protein-rich beer that was consumed as much for its food value as for its inebriating properties. The history of the use of opium, an addictive narcotic drug formed by the dried juice of the opium poppy plant, is also lengthy, dating back six thousand years to Mesopotamia (an area that is now Iraq), where Sumerians used the drug to treat many illnesses. The use of marijuana, an intoxicating drug derived from the hemp plant, also dates to about 4000 B.C.E. It was first used in China as an anesthetic, and later the Greeks and Romans employed it in treating indigestion and controlling muscle spasms. Coca leaves, the source of the powerful behavioral stimulant cocaine, have been chewed by South American Indians in the Andes mountains for thousands of years. By comparison, to-

Workers distill spirits in a Renaissance laboratory. Monks discovered the process of distillation during the Middle Ages.

bacco is a relative newcomer to the drug scene, having been smoked by American Indians for a few centuries before the arrival of European settlers.

Drugs have been worshiped and the plants from which they are derived called the "gifts of the gods." They have also been denounced as instruments of the devil. At various times each individual drug has been widely misunderstood by both those championing its use and those condemning it.

Although many of the volumes in this encyclopedia contain histories of individual drugs, *Drugs Through the Ages* will examine drug use from a broader perspective to demonstrate how all drugs relate to each other and to show how religious, political, medical, and societal opinions can alter our overall perception of any given drug.

The story of tobacco is a good example of just how interrelated the histories of different drugs can be. Tobacco smoking, a practice imported from the New World in the 16th century, immediately became popular in England and spread rapidly throughout Europe. Until then, the idea of inhaling the smoke of burning dried leaves must have seemed preposterous to Europeans.

Not surprisingly, experiments in smoking other plants containing psychoactive substances soon followed. For example, until the 16th century opium and cannabis (marijuana) were usually eaten. Soon both were being smoked on a widespread basis. In the 17th century opium was mixed with tobacco and exported from India to China, where millions quickly became addicted opium smokers. Thus tobacco, a medicinal herb the American Indians originally regarded as a gift from their Great Spirit deity, brought about a worldwide smoking epidemic.

Many factors, often seemingly unrelated, profoundly influence the role a drug plays in society. For example, the hypodermic needle, invented in 1853, enabled morphine, the principal narcotic chemical in opium, to be injected — a development that triggered an epidemic of morphine addiction.

The history of drug use is also a saga of taxation, prohibition, and criminal violence, as each society has struggled to control excess use and rampant profiteering. Yet history has not enlightened contemporary attitudes toward drugs as much as might be hoped. Drug use remains a powerful force in modern society. If we hope to understand why drugs are so abused today, or to sort through our own personal questions regarding them, the past is a good place to begin.

A statue depicts the 15th-century B.C.E. Egyptian pharaoh Amenhotep II offering a libation to a god. Drinking bouts sometimes lasted several days at Egyptian religious festivals.

CHAPTER 1

PREHISTORY
AND
ANCIENT HISTORY

The history of drugs begins with alcohol, which was the most widespread drug of ancient Asia, Europe, and Africa. Opium, a substance prepared from the milky juice of the poppy plant and from which such narcotics as morphine and heroin are derived, was first used many centuries before the beginning of the Common Era (C.E., equivalent to A.D.). Hallucinogens — mushrooms, cacti, or herbs first eaten by primitive peoples who, in their search for food, were willing to taste almost anything — were the first drugs used in North and South America, followed by coca and tobacco.

The Earliest Uses of Drugs

The varying characteristics of these early drugs inspired widely different uses. Alcohol was first used as a beverage to accompany a meal. It encouraged conversation, which qualified it from the start as a social drug. Hallucinogens had mystical effects and produced overpowering visions that seemed like direct visitations of gods. The depressant action of opium made it an important painkiller. All these drugs played a role in primitive folk medicine.

23

Myths About Alcohol

Egyptian carvings from 4500 B.C.E. depict the making of wine, which was considered a gift from the god Osiris. Beer and wine were dietary staples. One ancient inscription directs good mothers to provide their schoolboy sons with three loaves of bread and two jars of beer every day. The carvings also record that in 1198 B.C.E. the soldiers of Pharaoh Ramses III received a daily ration of wine.

However, in another Egyptian inscription, a teacher warns a wayward student against the abominations of wine and fears that the student has become like a broken oar, which cannot steer a steady course.

Wine making was part of Chinese culture before 2000 B.C.E. In 2285 B.C.E. a man was banished for inventing an alcoholic drink from rice. One Chinese legend from the year

A painting from an Egyptian tomb shows winemakers treading harvested grapes to the left of wine-storage jugs. Wine was widely used in ancient Egypt and was thought to be a gift from the god Osiris.

The painting on this Greek kylix (drinking cup) from the 6th century B.C.E. depicts the god Dionysus dancing. The Greeks sometimes became extremely intoxicated at Dionysian rites, but alcohol abuse was not a widespread problem in ancient Greece.

2150 B.C.E. tells of two royal astronomers, He and Ho, who got drunk and failed to predict an eclipse. The prince declared that through their drunkenness they "allowed the regulations of Heaven to get into disorder . . . and the Sun and the Moon did meet harmoniously." For neglect of their duty, the two unfortunate astronomers were put to death.

A Chinese legend from the 18th century B.C.E. tells of a ruler, Kia, who provided his favorite concubine with a "splendid palace, and in the parks which surrounded it, a lake of wine at which three thousand men drank at the sound of a drum." The great 6th-century B.C.E. philosopher and teacher Confucius decreed against such excesses, and monarchs in China and Japan later tried to encourage tea drinking as a substitute.

In ancient Mesopotamia, beer was used not only as a popular drink but also in temple ritual. Although taverns, often run by women, became gathering places for an increasingly complex society, the law strictly forbade the mixing of social and religious drinking. At around 1800 B.C.E. the ruler Hammurabi declared that any priestess found keeping a beer shop should be burned to death.

Phoenician sailors first brought wine to Greece around 800 B.C.E., although the Greeks attributed its arrival on their shores to their god Dionysus. The Greeks also believed that Dionysus was present in the wine, and they drank to a point of intoxication so they could feel the god's presence. The most common Greek drinking vessel was called a *kylix*. Often beautifully decorated, the kylix had two handles, allowing it to be passed from hand to hand, and a rim so broad that the drinker was almost forced to take a large swig. Dionysian revels were renowned for their unrestrained drinking. Even the philosopher Plato, who objected to drunkenness, made an exception for the Dionysian rites.

The Greek poet Homer, who probably lived during the 8th century B.C.E., alluded to the power of wine in various ways. In *The Odyssey*, Ulysses overcame the monstrous one-eyed Cyclops by getting him drunk and boring out his eye. In *The Iliad* the poet wrote of "the bewitching wine, which sets even a wise man to singing and to laughing gently and rouses him to dance and brings forth words which were better left unspoken."

Ancient Customs and Rituals

Alcohol inspired some curious and macabre customs and taboos in the ancient world. The 5th-century B.C.E. Greek historian Herodotus described a king who entertained his soldiers with an annual feast. At this feast only those soldiers who had slain a man in battle could drink the wine. In ancient Persia the king and his officials first discussed important matters when drunk, then later reviewed them when sober. If both conferences reached the same decisions, then the king would act.

In early Rome wine was scarce and reserved for the rich, or it was used for worship or medicinal purposes. But by Julius Caesar's day, in the 1st century B.C.E., the drinking of wine became fashionable, and it was not uncommon for guests to eat and drink until they were full, vomit, and then continue to eat and drink some more. For good or ill, the upper classes in every age are emulated. The practices of the Roman high society were copied by people in other lands, and alcoholism became a recognized problem throughout the Western world. Hastened by Caesar's Gallic conquests, vineyards were established throughout Western Europe. In ancient Britain, in about 90 C.E., the popular grape harvests threatened to supplant the production of crops that were desperately needed for food.

Campaigns against alcohol use have often been tried, but curbing the substances's intoxicating potential has not always

According to the Old Testament, after the Flood Noah planted a grapevine on Mount Ararat and was punished when he became drunk on wine that he made from its fruit. Although wine serves a ritual function in both the Jewish and the Christian faiths, the Bible cautions frequently against excessive drinking.

been the chief reason for the prohibition. For example, one of the reasons the prophet Muhammad prohibited drinking was to separate Muslim tradition as much as possible from Christian tradition, in which wine was a sacred symbol. Muhammad also undoubtedly knew that alcohol, because it dehydrates the body, increases one's need for water, an undesirable consequence in a desert land like the Arabian peninsula.

The Bible mentions liquor in many contexts. The book of Genesis states that Noah planted a vineyard shortly after the Flood receded, and "drank of the wine, and became drunk." The book of Leviticus warns Aaron and his sons against drinking in the temple, although wine was used in the temple service. Both the Old and New Testaments refer to wine as a festive and healing drink, but contain admonishments against excessive drinking. "Do not get drunk with wine, for that is debauchery," wrote Apostle Paul.

The New Testament records that shortly before his death, Christ shared a Passover dinner with his disciples, and said of the wine, "This is my blood." Wine is consumed in many modern Christian communion services as a symbolic representation of the blood of Christ.

A Persian woman smokes opium through a water pipe in this manuscript illustration. Opium was used mainly for medicinal purposes in the ancient world.

Discovering Opium

Opium had its beginnings in the Mediterranean region, in Sumeria around 4000 B.C.E. Its paramount use was medicinal. Crude opium was prepared simply by slashing open the unripe poppy pods and drying the milky juice that oozed out. Ancient peoples sucked this bitter narcotic in lozenges, sniffed it, drank it, and ate it, but no one smoked opium until thousands of years later. The famous 5th-century B.C.E. Greek physician Hippocrates cited opium's therapeutic powers but in his day it was not considered one of the most important medicinal drugs.

Hemp, the plant from which marijuana is derived, was first used for making rope, perhaps as early as 4000 B.C.E. in

China. Hempen rope and cloth are among the plant's most important contributions to the civilized world. They were used for making ship's rigging, baskets, horse blankets, and altar cloths, and, in the 19th century, for covering the wagons of the American pioneers. Hemp seeds were a nutritious food for early peoples, and most ancient Old World cultures also used hemp for medical purposes. In India, hemp was claimed to control dandruff and relieve venereal disease, whooping cough, and tuberculosis.

The earliest evidence of hemp's use as an intoxicant also comes from China, although the dates cited vary from 2000 B.C.E. to 500 B.C.E. Its psychoactivity was also known early in India. The *Rig-Veda,* the Hindu book of hymns compiled about four thousand years ago, describes cannabis as a divine nectar, the favorite drink of Indra, lord of the heavens. An especially sacred preparation of the drug called *bhang* was consumed in candy or tea. Like opium, cannabis was eaten or drunk, but not widely smoked in India until the 16th century.

Although hemp was seldom used in the ancient world for its hallucinogenic properties, the Greeks occasionally gave it to guests, and drank it with wine and myrrh, an aromatic resin. Herodotus described a bath indulged in by the Scythians, horsemen from central Asia. They made a booth of animal pelts, placed hot stones and hemp seeds in a dish inside the booth, and then became "high" on the smoky vapor.

Fly Agaric

One of the oldest hallucinogens of both the Old and New Worlds is fly agaric, an exotic red mushroom with white flecks, once thought to be not only holy but an actual god in its own right. Fly agaric produced hallucinations and delirium, sometimes alternating with convulsions or depressive trances. In ancient India an elaborate cult developed around an intoxicating substance called *soma*; many scholars believe soma was made from fly agaric. The *Rig-Veda* contains hundreds of references to soma.

Fly agaric is native to many northern areas with temperate climates. Indians in northwestern Canada and near Lake Superior in Michigan knew about the "red-top mushroom" and associated it and other mushrooms with thunder and lightning.

The Peyote Cactus and Other Psychedelics

The peyote cactus of Mexico is an equally ancient and powerful hallucinogen, although not as widespread as fly agaric. Peyote's ceremonial and medicinal use dates back to the 1st century B.C.E. When the Spanish conquered Mexico in the 1500s, they condemned the use of peyote but never succeeded in stamping out the ritualistic use of the drug in the native religion. The woolly crown of the peyote cactus was cut off and dried into what is now called a "mescal button." Like mushrooms, mescal buttons can be stored indefinitely.

Mexico has the richest diversity of hallucinogenic plants in the world. Peyote is the most important of these, but 24 different species of sacred mushrooms, known to the Aztecs as *teonanacatl*, are still used there today. Fanciful mushroom-shaped stone carvings unearthed in Guatemala, some of which may be dated back three thousand years, may have been used in worship of these "little flowers of the gods."

The crown of the peyote cactus is harvested from the Mexican desert during the Huichol tribe's peyote pilgrimage in 1968. Peyote's ceremonial and medicinal use dates back to the 1st century B.C.E.

The hallucinogenic experience was usually a group venture. Often a *shaman*, a wise, priestlike medicine man or woman, would guide and interpret the visions. The ceremony surrounding the drug usually had a serious theme, such as healing a sick child or preventing a bad harvest. Sometimes puberty rites occasioned a person's first use of a hallucinogen, but these substances were rarely given to children.

Coca

The principal drug of ancient Peru was the stimulant coca. Long before their conquest by the Incas during the three centuries before the Spanish invasion, Peruvian Indians chewed coca leaves to increase strength and appease hunger. Coca chewing probably originated in the Amazon region and spread through northern South America. It was sacred to the Incas, who restricted its use to ceremonial rites. It was not then the common, daily stimulant it is for thousands of Andean Indians today. Incan religion pictured the divine essence of the plant as a beautiful woman. Coca was so important to the Incas that a Spanish conqueror observed: "If there were no coca, there would be no Peru."

Limits of Abuse

Of all these drugs, alcohol is the only one with an obvious record of abuse in the ancient world. Why? Early on, alcohol lost any exclusively sacred associations. It was easy to obtain and inexpensive, and it appealed to all social classes. Then, too, wine making was within the grasp of anyone owning a parcel of land.

Religious beliefs and taboos prevented the abuse of many other drugs. Faithful worshipers respected their sacred power. Many drugs were complicated to prepare or unpleasant to ingest, or were used only for medicinal purposes. Some did not allow people to function normally under their influence. Finally, most drugs were used only in group settings, a factor that may have reduced the chances of abuse.

An engraving of an outdoor medieval pharmacy depicts workers making medicines from plants. Although early Christian doctrine discouraged medical research, a few monasteries did establish medical facilities where psychoactive drugs were used as anesthetics.

CHAPTER 2

THE MIDDLE AGES:
476–1400

Knights in chain mail, fairy-tale castles, gold-illuminated manuscripts — romantic images like these make the Middle Ages (approximately 476–1400) seem as remote from the 20th century as the ancient world. Yet the Middle Ages had a profound influence on the present. The Catholic church grew during this period until its wealth and power surpassed that of any king. The Church established many divinity schools, which today are some of the world's great universities. Monasteries, the communal residences of orders of monks, kept Western learning alive for many centuries. The Church built magnificent Romanesque and Gothic cathedrals, influencing Western architecture for centuries to come. It also planted acres and acres of vineyards. In fact, many monasteries had their own wineries, some of which still produce outstanding wines.

Drunken Feasts and Brawls

Alcohol was the most widely used drug during the Middle Ages, just as it had been in the ancient world. There are numerous accounts from the period of drunken feasts and ensuing brawls, and records of thousands of gallons of beer and ale consumed at parties. King Edmund I of England was killed in a brawl in 946 because his nobles were too drunk to defend him. An account of the medieval Feast of the Ass notes that "drunkenness and wanton singing universally prevailed both among the clergy and the laity."

Indeed, the clergy, those people who had been ordained in the Church, had a reputation for especially heavy drinking. Extensive church vineyards produced far more wine than was needed for religious sacraments. Also, monasteries functioned as inns and taverns, and church law required that priests be generous hosts.

Essential Tools of Witchcraft

While the clergy were tending vineyards and stocking the monastery wine cellars, a less reputable element of the population was cultivating other drugs. Witchcraft was on the rise, and three herbs from a group of hallucinogenic flowering plants called the nightshade family — henbane, belladonna, and mandrake — became essential tools of that dark trade. Substances in these "hexing herbs" blocked out all sense of reality, elicited wild behavior, and produced a deep sleep, after which one remembered nothing. Ointments brewed from these herbs could be absorbed through the skin.

The Egyptians had known about henbane as early as 1500 B.C.E. It was probably the drug Homer had in mind in *The Iliad* when he describes how Helen of Troy drugged her guests. In the Middle Ages the crushed seeds of the henbane plant were added to beer to make it more intoxicating.

Belladonna, meaning "beautiful lady," derived its name from its sap, which was sought by fashionable Greek and Italian women. The sap dilated the pupils of their eyes, producing a dreamy stare that was considered quite beautiful. Belladonna was often added to the wine at orgies and was probably more responsible than was alcohol for the uncontrolled excesses that occurred at those feasts.

Mandrake was notorious in the Middle Ages for the shape of its roots as much as for its narcotic properties. The mandrake root usually branches in two parts, and it sometimes resembled a human form. Around those twisted dark roots a wealth of superstitions and myths were woven. The plant was alleged to shriek when pulled from the ground, and suppos-

34

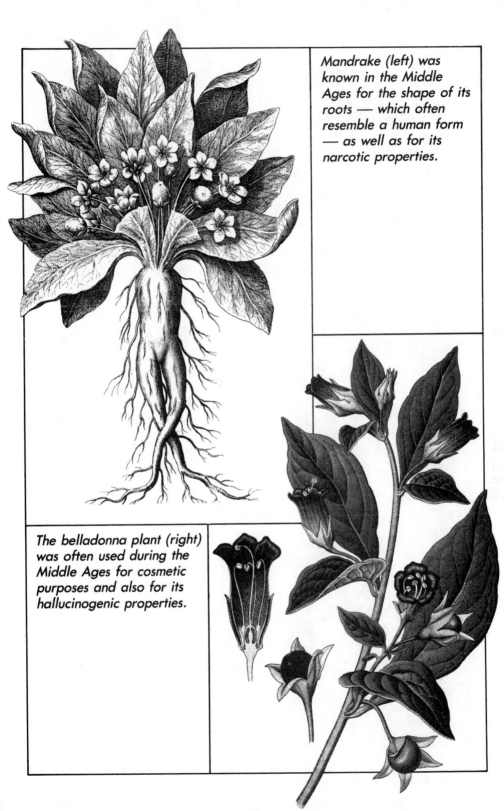

Mandrake (left) was known in the Middle Ages for the shape of its roots — which often resemble a human form — as well as for its narcotic properties.

The belladonna plant (right) was often used during the Middle Ages for cosmetic purposes and also for its hallucinogenic properties.

edly only black dogs could unearth it. Another myth held that it could grow only under a gallows. Many of these beliefs were not generally dispelled until the 16th century.

Lingering Myths and Superstitions

To a large extent the folklore of witchcraft and the fear these hallucinogenic drugs generated have never completely died. The familiar image of a Halloween witch flying on a broomstick has its origins in this period. The hexing herbs often did induce sensations of flying or of being transformed into animals such as black cats. One contemporary account reads: "The witches confess that on certain days and nights they anoint a staff and ride on it to the appointed place."

This German woodcut shows two witches mixing a potent brew. According to various texts written in the Middle Ages, hallucinogenic and poisonous plants were staples of potions allegedly prepared by witches.

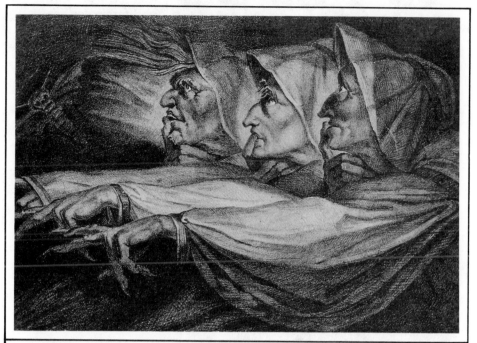

Three Witches, *by Johann Fussli. The image of a witch flying on a broomstick originated during the Middle Ages, perhaps because the ingestion of herbs such as henbane produced a sensation of flying.*

Psychoactive herbs may or may not have been involved in the witchcraft furor that broke out in Salem, Massachusetts, in the 17th century. One theory suggests that the town of Salem was plagued by ergot poisoning. Ergot, a fungus that attacks rye grain and causes hallucinations when eaten, contains lysergic acid, one of the basic compounds in the modern hallucinogen LSD.

Although the use of psychoactive herbs has often been associated with such mystical practices as ancient Indian tribal ceremonies and medieval witchcraft, it should be noted that one active ingredient in the hexing drugs — scopolamine — has had a modern application. From the 1930s through the 1950s many obstetricians in the United States and other Western countries prescribed scopolamine, called "twilight sleep," for women in childbirth. Knowing that the drug had no pain-killing properties, doctors nonetheless administered it because scopolamine had the dubious advantage of causing the

Marco Polo returned from his travels in China and fascinated the Venetian court with tales of his adventures. One of the most interesting stories involved a band of thieves whose leader rewarded them with *cannabis,* or hashish.

patient to remember nothing of her ordeal once the baby had been born and the drug's effects had worn off.

Cannabis (marijuana) is another drug that did not escape the legend making of the Middle Ages. One such tale, which has persisted with enormous influence well into the 20th century, involved a bloodthirsty 11th-century Persian ruler named Hasan. Supposedly he fed his followers large amounts of cannabis, which enabled them to conduct murderous rampages on behalf of their leader. The Arabic word for cannabis, *hashish,* is for this reason the source of the word *assassin,* and this story about the "old man of the mountain" provides the foundation for marijuana's reputation as a "killer weed" that turns its users into murderers.

A version of this tale was brought to the West by the 13th-century Venetian traveler Marco Polo. When he visited Hasan's mountain palace, natives in the region described for him Hasan's beautiful palace garden, called "Paradise." According to them, Hasan had indeed drugged many young men with "a certain potion" and then brought them into his magical "Paradise." After enjoying the visual and sexual delights of this "Paradise," the youths were willing to murder Hasan's enemies in order to get back in. There certainly were drugs involved in this account, but they were probably opium and wine rather than cannabis.

It is not surprising that Marco Polo's story became so distorted. Psychoactive drugs have always been subject to exaggerations and misunderstandings.

The discovery of the New World by Christopher Columbus in 1492 was one of many achievements that occurred during the Renaissance. The American continents would be a source and a market for drugs.

CHAPTER 3

THE AGE OF DISCOVERY:
1440–1750

The years between 1440 and 1750 were rich with exploration and discovery in every field, from art and music to science and medicine. The printing press was invented in 1440, and numerous botanical books were among the first volumes printed. As a result information about psychoactive herbs became more widely available, and many ancient superstitions and myths were refuted. Travel books also began to appear, describing the strange flora and fauna of the New World for fascinated readers. New liquors and new psychoactive plants expanded the choices of available drugs.

Moderation Versus Abstinence

The drinking of beer and wine was quite heavy throughout this period. Some notable authorities began to voice concern. Martin Luther and John Calvin, two prominent leaders of the Protestant Reformation, pleaded for moderation, while, in the 17th century, a new Protestant sect, the Baptists, advocated total abstinence. During the first half of the 17th century King James I of England and his successor, Charles I, attempted to enforce strict punishments for drunkenness, but neither monarch succeeded in enforcing sobriety.

WARE BILD NIS CAL LAND P ZV GENF

NVS IOHA VINI WE PFARRE IN SOPHO

B—H 157

The 16th-century religious leader John Calvin advocated strict penalties for drunkenness — which he considered sinful — and wanted public drinking places closed. Beer and wine were the favorite alcoholic beverages in his time, but whiskey was also available.

In the 17th and early 18th centuries, a tremendous increase in the consumption of beer, wine, and distilled spirits such as brandies and liqueurs occurred throughout Europe. Whiskey and gin were also becoming increasingly popular. Whiskey was first produced some time before 1500, probably in Scotland, and derives its name from the Scots Gaelic phrase *uisge beatha*, meaning "water of life." Gin was invented by the Dutch physician Sylvius in 1672. Like brandy, both drinks were initially very expensive and used solely as medicines.

The Gin Epidemic

The Industrial Revolution, which began in the 1700s, released forces that transformed the nation of England from a rural country into an urban one. The period from 1750 to 1850 also produced a series of depressing social results — crowded tenements, brutal working conditions, terribly low wages, and stretches of high unemployment. Gin, brought over from Holland by British soldiers, became the drink of the poor, their solace for a hard and miserable existence. Cheap gin was sold everywhere in London and was given instead of wages by some employers to their workers. The result was a period plagued by what is known as the gin epidemic. Legal efforts to control the abuse of gin proved largely ineffective, and one especially stringent law provoked widespread bootlegging and violent protests known as gin riots.

In the American colonies, alcoholic drinks were widely available. The staid Puritan settlers did not altogether disapprove of drinking in moderation but dealt harshly with those who drank to excess. In fact, drunkards were put in the stocks or compelled to wear a large letter "D" around their necks. The colonists primarily drank fermented cider, beer, and ale. Dutch settlers established the New World's first distillery on Staten Island in 1640. On the West Coast, Spanish priests planted numerous vineyards, laying the foundation for California's wine industry.

The American colonies were also involved in the rum trade. The colonies imported molasses from the sugar cane plantations of the West Indies and refined it to make rum. The rum was then traded in Africa for slaves. Human lives were thus bartered and sacrificed merely to obtain the "demon rum." Whiskey gradually replaced rum as the most popular alcoholic beverage in the United States shortly after Irish and Scottish settlers introduced it in the early 19th century.

Slaves are auctioned off in western Africa. Colonial slave traders often used rum rather than money to buy their human merchandise.

"The Hellish Practice" of Smoking

An Italian travel book published in 1565 called *Stories of the New World* contained this description of a new drug — tobacco—and the strange practice of smoking:

> They [Guatemalan Indians] then take the stalk of a certain plant and wrap one of the dried leaves around it, and thus make something resembling a pipe, one end of which they hold over the fire while they apply the other end to their lips, and inhale the smoke or vapor. Thus they fill mouth, gullet, and the whole head with the powerful fumes until at last their monstrous lust is sated. . . . It is hardly possible for one who has not experienced it to realize how injurious, how poisonous is this hellish practice.

Obviously the author did not recommend importing this foreign weed.

The circumstances under which a drug is introduced in society can exert a powerful influence on whether it is accepted. When Sir Walter Raleigh, the 16th-century English courtier and piratical explorer, returned to England from the colony of Virginia in 1586, he extolled the virtues of tobacco. Already an addicted smoker, Raleigh claimed that tobacco smoking promoted good health among the Virginia colonists and was revered by the Indians of the East Coast, who had used the plant for many centuries.

Because of the Europeans' fascination with imports from the New World and admiration of heroic adventurers, tobacco smoking quickly became a fad in England. Even Queen Elizabeth I tried it. By 1641 there were 7,000 smoke shops in London alone. In just a few decades tobacco smoking had become common among all social classes in Europe.

During this period people smoked pipes rather than cigarettes. There were silver pipes, clay pipes, and homemade pipes fashioned from walnut shells and straws. Many pipes were more than a foot long. At taverns a single pipe was often passed from hand to hand, serving many people. Tobacco clubs formed so that men could smoke at the dinner table, a practice considered improper at home. King Frederick I of Prussia held formal tobacco parties, surrounded by all his generals and ministers of state.

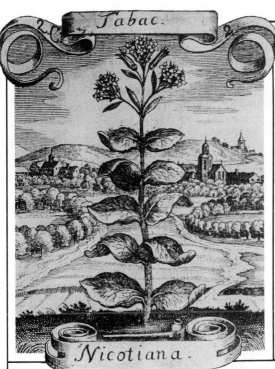

Tabac.

Nicotiana.

Left: Use of the tobacco plant was well established in the New World by the time Columbus arrived. Below: An 18th-century engraving shows an Indian smoking. Indians believed tobacco to be therapeutic, and many of them were addicted to it.

The American Colonies.

The Good Pinch *by Honoré Daumier. Snuff does not contain tar, a toxic substance present in cigarettes, but it does contain nicotine.*

"The Enchanted Herb"

In the late 1600s snuff, made from powdered tobacco, became popular. Often richly perfumed, the powder was inhaled through the nose. Snuff originated in France, where it was an upper-class habit and considered more delicate than pipe smoking. Fashionable young men and women at the French court carried dainty silver snuffboxes. Although Louis XIV of France disapproved of snuff, it was so prevalent in the royal court that he could not effectively forbid its use. The king's German sister-in-law, Duchess Elisabeth of Orléans, was one of the few members of the court who shared Louis's distaste for snuff, as a letter to her stepsister reveals:

> There is nothing in the world that I hate like snuff; it gives people dirty noses, makes them talk through their noses, and smell horribly. I have seen people here who once had the sweetest breath in the world, and after they took to snuff, in six months they stank like goats. There is nothing, I think, nastier than taking snuff and getting one's nose just as if — excuse the phrase — one had tumbled into a muck heap. Our King likes it no more

than I do, but all his children and grandchildren take to it, without caring for displeasing the King. It is better to take no snuff at all than a little, for it is certain that he who takes a little will soon take much, and that is why they call it "the enchanted herb," for those who take it are so taken by it that they cannot go without it; so take care of yourself, dear Louise!

The Tobacco Plague Begins

When the deadly bubonic plague ravaged London in 1665 and Vienna in 1679, some physicians suggested that tobacco might offer some protection. Schoolboys at Eton, England's exclusive boarding school, had to smoke every morning to "disinfect" themselves. In addition, kings and princes throughout Europe began to see tobacco as a rich source of revenue and to tax it heavily. Taxation did little to damage the substance's popularity, however, and people opposed to tobacco began to view it as a plague in its own right.

Tobacco spread more quickly than any other drug in history. Why? The first answer is simple: nicotine, a substance contained in tobacco, is a highly addictive psychoactive drug. Second, in the 1600s and 1700s smoking itself was a completely new practice and did not have to overcome established laws or conventions. The new technique was also orally satisfying and relatively easy to learn. Furthermore, after regular imports and European cultivation began, tobacco was cheap.

The beans of the cacao tree, shown here in an illustration from a Mexican manuscript, yielded a mildly psychoactive powder that, when mixed with sugar and water, appealed greatly to the Spanish conquerors of Latin America.

A scene from plague-torn 17th-century Europe. Some physicians during this time prescribed tobacco as a preventive measure against the bubonic plague epidemics in Vienna and London.

Chachaletto

New World explorers came upon several other drugs in addition to tobacco. In South America Spanish explorers encountered coca, a drug that did not become well known in Europe until the late 19th century. In Mexico the Spanish settlers encountered peyote and rejected it on moral grounds. Condemning the use of peyote as pagan, Spanish priests required potential Indian converts to swear off all use of the hallucinogen.

Not all the New World products discovered by the Spanish were unwelcome. In 1519, when the Aztecs in Mexico offered Hernando Cortez, the leader of the Spanish conquest, some of their precious cacao beans, the Spanish found a substance they could accept. The Aztecs concocted a cold, bitter preparation from the cacao tree's seeds, and reserved it for gods and royalty. The Spanish added sugar and hot water, and *chachaletto* was born. Hot chocolate was not known to any Europeans except the Spanish until the early 18th century, when it became the rage in Europe and Colonial America, often outselling coffee and tea.

48

The Stimulant Caffeine

Two other caffeine-containing drugs — coffee and tea — entered the European market before chocolate. Coffee originated in Ethiopia, according to legend, at least as early as the 600s, but its use did not become widespread until many centuries later, when it became popular among people in Arab countries. Like other drugs, coffee's psychoactive properties may have been discovered by accident. One old legend claims that an Arabian goatherd noticed that his flock stayed awake for long periods of time after eating the berries of certain plants. The goatherd boiled the plant's berries and served the drink to local monks, supposedly enabling them to remain awake for late-night services.

Coffee eventually became a standard social drink in Muslim countries, which prohibit the use of alcohol. As a result, coffeehouses soon became popular gathering places for animated conversations about politics and religion. In 1511 the governor of the Arabian holy city of Mecca ordered them closed, fearful that the houses generated too much dissent and threatened the regime. The edict could not overcome the popularity of the coffeehouses and was not in effect for very long.

In the mid-20th century, Middle Eastern men congregate in a coffeehouse. In 1511 the governor of Mecca gave an order to close the city's coffeehouses, which have long been gathering places in many Muslim countries. The edict, however, could not overcome the popularity of the coffeehouses and was unenforceable.

A Japanese print shows a woman holding a teacup. Tea was first used in Japan around 800 C.E., mainly for medicinal purposes. The traditional tea ceremony was developed by a Japanese emperor in 1484 and remains popular in the 20th century.

Coffee spread from Arab countries to Italy during the first half of the 17th century. There the clergy viewed it with suspicion until the pope himself tried it and found it to his liking. From Italy the use of coffee traveled slowly northward, greeted with either praise or condemnation from physicians, who were the first to proclaim about the new drug. "A vile and worthless foreign novelty," wrote one French physician. Another declared that coffee aided "menstrual problems, promoted urine flow, strengthened the heart . . . and relieved migraine." By 1675 coffee had been introduced to London, where coffeehouses soon began to stimulate political discussions, just as they had in Arab countries. These often rebellious discussions threatened King Charles II, who closed three thousand of the coffeehouses. By the time they reopened, tea had become the national drink of England.

The Origins of Tea

The legend of tea's origins as a drink dates back to 2737 B.C.E., when a Chinese philosopher noticed a pleasing fragrance after some tea leaves had accidentally fallen into his cooking pot. The philosopher tasted the resulting beverage and later wrote about his remarkable discovery: "Tea is better than wine for it does not lead to intoxication, neither does it cause a man to say foolish things. . . . It is better than water for it does not carry disease." By boiling water for their tea, the Chinese unknowingly killed harmful bacteria. Over the centuries the Chinese cultivated many varieties of tea, drinking it plain or with salt, or transforming it into a meal by adding butter and barley or oatmeal.

A tea plantation in China. Tea's origins date back to the 28th century B.C.E., when a Chinese philosopher noticed a pleasing fragrance after some tea leaves had fallen into his pot of hot water. The Chinese have cultivated many varieties of tea over the centuries.

The rebellious political discussions that took place in British coffeehouses during the late 17th century prompted King Charles II to close 3,000 of them. By the time they reopened some 50 years later, tea was the national drink of England.

Tea was first brought to Europe in 1610 by Dutch traders. An exuberant Dutch physician, believing that coffee and tea could speed blood circulation, wrote: "We advise tea for the whole nation and for every nation. We advise men and women to drink tea daily; hour by hour if possible; beginning with ten cups a day, and increasing the dose to the utmost quantity the stomach can contain and the kidneys can eliminate."

The British needed no doctor's encouragement to fire their enthusiasm for tea, which was first introduced to that country around 1666. At first many British people welcomed tea as a substitute for wine. In fact, it was sometimes marketed as a cure for the nation's growing drinking problem. One bit of verse in a popular magazine read:

> From boist'rous Wine I fled to gentle tea,
> For calms compose us after storms at sea; . . .
> Yea even the ills from coffee it repairs,
> Disclaims its vices and its virtues shares.

In the mid-1700s, the British government imposed heavy taxes on tea. By then the British had surrendered their hearts to the drink, and the teapot was the center of every British hearth. Faced with the prospect of having to give up this favorite indulgence, the British smuggled great quantities of tea into the country from the Continent. The American colonists did likewise — to them, the tea tax represented unfair British control over one of life's essential pleasures and yet one more intolerable instance of "taxation without representation." In 1773 patriots in Boston made their objections known in unmistakable terms by dumping large quantities of tea into the harbor, an act that became known as the Boston Tea Party.

Beer Street, an engraving by William Hogarth. Alcoholism in 18th-century England was no longer due solely to wine and beer — by 1792 the British were importing 10 million gallons of Dutch gin annually.

CHAPTER 4

THE SCIENTIFIC AGE
PART I: 1750–1870

Scientific knowledge about drugs increased significantly in the years between 1750 and 1870. In 1753 Carolus Linnaeus, a Swedish naturalist and physician, published his new system of plant classification. He gave two Latin names to each plant, a generic name and a species name, a useful method of identification now universally employed in botany. Linnaeus estimated that the plant kingdom contained about 10,000 species. Twentieth-century botanists believe there may be as many as 700,000 species, many of them psychoactive plants not yet discovered.

Distilling Pure Psychoactive Compounds

During the 18th and 19th centuries botanists and chemists grew more interested in finding the substances in psychoactive plants that produced their powerful effects. They sought the active compounds causing the effects that people of the Middle Ages had believed to be magical. In 1806 a German pharmacist, Friedrich Serturner, isolated the first pure psychoactive plant compound — morphine — from the opium poppy.

Pure psychoactive compounds have always posed a problem for humankind. Overuse of distilled liquor, another pure drug, had already been aggravating Europe's alcoholism

Carolus Linnaeus traveled 4,600 miles through Scandinavia studying plant life before publishing his system of plant classification in 1753. His work encouraged other botanists to search for psychoactive compounds in the species he had catalogued.

problem for some time. Public drunkenness, along with unemployment and urban overcrowding, persisted in England throughout the new Industrial Age. In 1751 another legislative attempt to control London's gin shops was effective in getting drunks off the streets, but much of the population still drank to excess. In fact, by 1792 the British were importing 10 million gallons of Dutch gin annually.

In the new United States, attitudes toward drinking were developing that would continue up to the time of Prohibition and even beyond. Generally, they were of two extremes. On one hand, there were the ways of the frontier, where corn "likker" was cheap and strong, and a man was respected if he could swig great amounts of it and still hold himself upright. Above all, the frontier championed rugged individualism. For example, when the federal government tried to enforce a whiskey excise tax in 1794, citizens in western Pennsylvania tarred and feathered the revenue collectors. This episode became known as the Whiskey Rebellion.

On the other hand, the nation's Protestant churches increasingly espoused sobriety and abstinence and considered alcoholism a moral weakness. Temperance was preached as a logical corollary to the Gospel, and by 1835 more than 35,000 ministers had shown their support for it by signing a pledge of abstinence. By 1855 more than 1 million Americans had joined a temperance organization. One dramatic result of this movement was a considerable decline in the consumption of liquor. By 1849 Americans were drinking 75% less alcohol than they had just 20 years earlier.

The Opium Epidemic

It was opium, however, and not alcohol, that first crippled an entire nation with addiction. Beginning in the 17th century under the Ming Dynasty, and culminating in the middle of the 19th century, tens of millions of Chinese became opium addicts. The opium came from India, where it had been cultivated and used in folk medicine for centuries with few problems of addiction. But in China, where opium was often mixed with tobacco and smoked, use of the drug was personal, informal, and unregulated. Soon it had invaded all social classes and especially endangered the health of the poor, who often chose opium over food when they could not afford both.

A 19th-century American woodcut advocating temperance dramatically highlights the corrupting powers of drink. The early 19th-century temperance crusade was remarkably successful — by 1849 Americans were drinking 75% less alcohol than they had drunk just 20 years earlier.

DR.C.V. GIRARD'S GINGER BRANDY.

"A CERTAIN CURE" for Cholera Colic Cramps Dysentery, Chills & Fever, is a delightful & healthy beverage.

FOR SALE HERE.

An 1861 advertisement for ginger brandy shows two hunters administering the beverage to an ill comrade. Many advertisements in the 19th century falsely claimed that medicines containing a large percentage of alcohol could cure a variety of ailments.

Never in the history of drug use have so many people been affected so drastically. Three factors were responsible for this epidemic addiction in China. First, the enormous appeal of smoking tobacco, which had begun in the mid-1600s, led in turn to the smoking of opium in China. In India, opium had always been eaten, a form of ingestion much less addictive. Second, opium was immediately accepted in China by doctors and the upper classes. Lastly, the drug had no traditional cultural role. As was the case with tobacco in Europe, there was no history to guide people in their use of the drug or to warn them of the danger of abuse.

Every Chinese social class succumbed. Opium dens pro-liferated, and some of them were quite elegant. Doctors smoked while consulting with their patients. Businessmen passed a ceremonial pipe during business transactions. Women smoked. Tired peasants relaxed with a pipe at the end of the day. By the 1840s there were an estimated 1 million users in China.

As early as 1729, China had passed the first of many ultimately ineffective edicts against the use of opium. During this time the East India Company, formed by the British in 1600, monopolized the prosperous opium trade. In 1839 Chinese authorities, alarmed at their country's growing ad-diction problem, seized a supply of smuggled opium from the British and destroyed it. This action triggered the Opium War, which lasted from 1839 to 1842. During the decade after the war several unequal treaties were signed between Britain and China. Some British argued that opium actually benefited the Chinese and caused no more harm than alcohol or tobacco. The Chinese emperor beseeched the British to end the opium trade. Women's groups in England and the Anglican church campaigned strongly against it, making the opium trade a highly charged moral issue. In time opium addiction in China subsided as trade with Britain ended, and by 1900 only a few wealthy Chinese still maintained their expensive habit.

Heroin and Morphine Abuse

China's drug problems were far removed from the United States until the 1850s, when opium first arrived in San Fran-cisco, along with Chinese "coolies," unskilled laborers who helped build America's western railroads. Soon, American prejudice against opium smoking became intertwined with a general prejudice against the Chinese. In 1875 California passed a narcotics control act to limit opium use. Other states soon passed similar measures, and in 1909 the United States prohibited all imports of opium.

But just as the use of opium was declining, another, more potent drug—heroin—was introduced into the United States. Derived from morphine in 1898, heroin was easy to admin-ister and easy for drug dealers to conceal, because of its lack of strong odor. Stiff federal prohibitions eventually forced the

An opium den in New York City during the late 19th century. When Chinese laborers entered the United States in the 1850s, they brought with them the practice of opium smoking. This custom exacerbated already existing racial prejudice against the Chinese.

drug market underground, and today's narcotics underworld was born.

As mentioned in the Author's Preface, the invention of the hypodermic needle in 1853 also had a profound impact on the history of drug use. Initially, it was used to inject wounded soldiers with the painkiller morphine during the Crimean War (1853–56), the U.S. Civil War (1861–65), and the Franco-Prussian War (1870–71). As a result, many veterans of those wars became morphine addicts. Once again, because society had no precedent for treating or even understanding addiction, abuse was almost inevitable.

"The Beloved Herb, Tobacco"

Tobacco maintained its worldwide popularity during the late 18th and early 19th centuries. In country after country, governmental restrictions were abandoned, until the only regulations against smoking concerned possible fire hazards. In many countries the clergy smoked and took snuff. Women had succumbed to the habit for some time, and one doctor even endorsed their smoking, saying: "It is a glorious venture when a woman takes heart to smoke a pipe of tobacco. Her charming sex has an equal right with men." Some people, however, continued to be alarmed at the increasing consumption of tobacco. A popular writer of the day commented:

> Now things have come to such a pass (Lord have mercy on us!) that we poor people of the Old World get something from the New World which right soon packs us off into the next world. Especially is this true of the beloved herb tobacco, a noble plant, but sore misused among us.

At the end of the 18th century a new mode of smoking became fashionable. Called *cigarros* in Spanish, they resembled the simple cigars that Indians in Mexico, Guatemala, and the West Indies had been smoking for centuries. The use of cigars spread slowly but surely throughout Europe. The cigar remained more popular than snuff or pipe tobacco until the end of the 19th century, when it too was replaced by another fashionable smoking tool—the cigarette.

Sigmund Freud, the founder of psychoanalysis, was so enthusiastic about the therapeutic powers of cocaine that he prescribed it as a cure for the morphine addiction of his close friend Ernst von Fleischl-Marxow. Ironically, Fleischl-Marxow became dependent upon cocaine, and he subsequently died from its poisonous effects.

CHAPTER 5

THE SCIENTIFIC AGE
PART II: 1870–1920

During the last decades of the 19th century, European and American societies distinguished between those psychoactive drugs that were socially and medically acceptable and those that were not. Cocaine and cigarettes were allowed, alcohol and snuff were not. During this period scientific understanding of psychoactive drugs did manage to advance somewhat, though exaggerated hopes and prejudices — to say nothing of addiction—persisted.

Although alcohol has never entirely lacked enthusiastic devotees at any time in its history, temperance movements in Europe and the United States managed to make drinking very unpopular in the late 19th century. Many people believed that even moderate drinking was wrong and that anyone who did drink was certainly not respectable. Many drinkers frequented saloons, which were visited exclusively by males and often offered the additional temptations of gambling and prostitution.

"Of the Women, By the Women"

American women played a crucial role in advancing the cause of temperance. They were gradually becoming better educated, and their interests were expanding. Many Victorian men and women believed that there were separate spheres for the two sexes, and that the woman's sphere was the home.

Women argued that drinking destroyed the home in a number of ways. For them, a responsible, sober husband was an essential part of a healthy domestic life.

Shortly before Christmas in 1873, in Hillsboro, Ohio, one hundred well-to-do matrons appeared at the town's saloons, where they knelt in prayer and asked the saloons' owners to close the establishments. The vigil, which went on for several weeks, was soon joined by women in other states. The idea gained popularity and widespread newspaper coverage. Within six months three thousand saloons had closed, at least temporarily. In 1874 the Women's Christian Temperance Union (WCTU) formed, soon to become the largest women's association in 19th-century America. Frances Willard, an influential president of the WCTU, declared that the temperance cause was "of the women, by the women, but for humanity."

Men found it difficult to object to a cause embedded in such worthy sentiments. Certainly they found temperance a less threatening issue than giving women the right to vote. Also, the WCTU was quite conservative, espousing traditional roles for women. Some of the temperance leaders were married to prominent men. Few women were arrested during

The Women's Christian Temperance Union, a 1932 painting by Ben Shahn. Founded in 1874 in Cleveland, Ohio, the WCTU promoted total abstinence from alcohol. The organization is still active.

Carrie Nation, the WCTU's most controversial member, often used violent tactics in her attempts to close down saloons in Kansas. She was fined, arrested, and even shot at for her efforts.

the vigils, with the dramatic exception of Carrie Nation, the WCTU's most outspoken and controversial member. Dressed in her Sunday best, hatchet in hand, Carrie Nation wreaked havoc in barroom after barroom during the 1890s, shattering windows and smashing whiskey glasses. Most WCTU members disapproved of her tactics, feeling she brought their cause negative publicity.

Between 1846 and 1904 numerous states passed prohibition laws only to repeal them or modify them shortly thereafter. Yet pressure for nationwide prohibition continued to mount, supported mainly by Protestant churches, temperance organizations, and the Prohibition Party, which had been formed in 1869 for the primary purpose of working for laws that would outlaw the manufacture and sale of alcoholic beverages. By 1920, 14 states had adopted some form of prohibition. Then, at midnight on January 16, 1920, the Eighteenth (National Prohibition) Amendment went into effect. America's "noble experiment" had begun.

Ether: The Short-lived Epidemic

Many temperance groups in Europe advocated moderation rather than total prohibition. Churches held retreats at which church members signed pledges swearing to stay off liquor. In Ireland temperance advocates made the mistake of encouraging alcoholics to use ether as a substitute for gin, which had become so heavily taxed that the poor could no longer afford it. Ether, a liquid that was just beginning to be used in anesthesia, produced a "high" similar to that of alcohol, was inexpensive, and was easily available at pharmacies. In a short time ether was being abused by many of the nation's poor. In fact, by the 1890s, 8% of the population of the province of Ulster, Ireland, were "ethermaniacs." Besides

An 1845 advertisement for an exhibition of "laughing gas," or nitrous oxide. Gaseous intoxicants such as nitrous oxide and ether became popular substances of abuse when legislation in various countries had made liquor either too expensive or too difficult to obtain.

A late-19th-century advertisement for Coca-Cola promoted the beverage — which at that time contained cocaine — as a drink that "relieves exhaustion."

being addictive, ether is dangerously flammable and awkward to inhale. Therefore, when the price of gin came down, the ether epidemic ended abruptly.

Euphoria Over Coca and Cocaine

While politicians and middle-class women and men had debated the prohibition of alcohol at the end of the 19th century, coca and its derivative, cocaine, dominated the attention of physicians, artists, and intellectuals. Despite a few negative 16th-century reports from Spanish explorers, coca's reputation had slowly improved. Nineteenth-century travelers were impressed by the effectiveness of coca in relieving respiratory problems at high altitudes, suppressing the appetite, and increasing physical endurance. One observer wrote in 1846: "I am clearly of the opinion that moderate use of coca is not merely innocuous, but that it may even be very conducive to health." Only a few disagreed. A German physician, Eduard Poeppig, wrote in 1836 that the routine coca chewer was "the slave of his passion even more than the drunk" and "incapable of pursuing any serious goals in life." Nevertheless coca's enthusiasts, many of them highly respected physicians, continued to multiply.

Between 1855 and 1862, various German chemists isolated cocaine from coca leaves. Shortly thereafter an Italian chemist, Angelo Mariani, created a mixture of coca extract and wine that he called Vin Mariani. Soon doctors throughout Europe were recommending Vin Mariani for sore-throat complaints. Military physicians also expressed interest in cocaine's ability to enable armies to walk long distances without food or sleep. A British medical journal editorialized in 1876 that coca would be "a new stimulant and a new narcotic: two forms of novelty in excitement which our modern civilization is highly likely to esteem."

Euphoria about coca and cocaine reached its height in the 1870s and 1880s in both Europe and the United States. The American drug company Parke-Davis, as well as many influential physicians, promoted cocaine as a "cure" for addiction to morphine, opium, and alcohol. Parke-Davis also sold cocaine in cigarette form. In 1886 a Georgia pharmacist created the beverage Coca-Cola, which contained coca as its main active ingredient. Advertisements for coca products like the new soft drink appealed to "young persons afflicted with timidity in society." The *Louisville Medical News* called such concoctions "harmless remedies for the blues."

In 1884 two events focused further attention on cocaine. The first was the publication of the psychiatrist Sigmund Freud's article titled "Über Coca" ("On Coca"). Freud recommended coca or cocaine for a variety of illnesses and described his own use of the drug, which he apparently took orally with some regularity. Although "Über Coca" was intended as an objective scientific paper, Freud could not suppress his enthusiasm for his subject. He wrote that cocaine produced "exhilaration and lasting euphoria," and implied that the drug's effects were harmless. "Über Coca" influenced many otherwise doubtful physicians and prompted Parke-Davis and other drug companies to advertise cocaine as "the most important therapeutic discovery of the age."

Left: Not realizing its addictive potential, the renowned inventor Thomas Alva Edison mistakenly endorsed Vin Mariani for its medicinal properties, which turned out to be nonexistent.

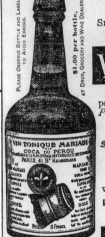

Right: Vin Mariani, a preparation that combined coca extract with wine, attracted many famous people as customers, including the author Jules Verne and Pope Leo XIII.

PLEASE OBSERVE BOTTLE AND LABEL, TO AVOID ERRORS.

$1.00 per bottle, AT DRUG, GROCERY AND WINE DEALERS.

For Body and Brain.

SINCE 30 YEARS ALL EMINENT PHYSICIANS RECOMMEND

VIN MARIANI

The original French Coca Wine; most popularly used tonic-stimulant in *Hospitals, Public and Religious Institutions* everywhere.

Nourishes   Fortifies   Refreshes

Strengthens entire system; most AGREEABLE, EFFECTIVE and LASTING Renovator of the Vital Forces.

Every test, strictly on its own merits, will prove its exceptional reputation.

PALATABLE AS CHOICEST OLD WINES.

Illustrated Book Sent Free, address:

MARIANI & CO., NEW YORK

TRIAL WILL CONVINCE

Cocaine as an Anesthetic

The second major event of 1884 concerning cocaine was the discovery by Carl Koller, a colleague of Freud, of the drug's usefulness as a topical (local) anesthetic in eye surgery. (Ether, the only other anesthetic at that time, produced negative side effects such as vomiting.) Moreover, eye surgery often required that patients be awake. Although cocaine anesthesia was dangerously toxic, Koller's discovery inspired further research. In the same year William Halsted of the Johns Hopkins Medical School invented nerve block, a way of deadening isolated sections of the body by injecting cocaine into nerves. Spinal anesthesia with cocaine was introduced in

1898. The following year saw the invention of novocaine, a synthetic substitute without toxic side effects.

With the endorsement of the medical profession, cocaine became a "respectable" drug — more respectable for women than alcohol. It was prescribed for neurasthenia, or nervous exhaustion, a common diagnosis at that time for a wide range of "female complaints," including headache, back pain, and depression. Angelo Mariani, inventor of Vin Mariani, expanded his market of coca preparations to include throat lozenges and tea and published a list of famous satisfied customers. The list included Thomas Edison, the tsar of Russia, the Prince of Wales, and even Pope Leo XIII!

Growing Realism About Cocaine

How could so many knowledgeable people have been so wrong? Other psychoactive drugs — alcohol, morphine, marijuana — have also passed through similar periods of exaggerated acclaim. New, less familiar drugs often offer hope of cures for addiction to older drugs. Even the late-20th-century medical profession has been guilty of overprescribing new drugs, notably tranquilizers such as Valium. Also, medicine in the late 19th century was a fledgling science. Doctors who often could do little more than try to make their dying patients comfortable had access to few effective drugs. Dosage amounts were not controlled, and few people appreciated how much more potent cocaine was than coca.

Gradually, evidence of cocaine's limitations and dangers mounted. Doctors were increasingly frustrated that cocaine dosages were so difficult to control and caused such different reactions in patients. Sigmund Freud saw Ernst von Fleischl-Marxow, who was a close friend and colleague, become the victim of cocaine addiction. Halsted, the inventor of nerve block anesthesia, also became addicted to cocaine. In fact, because of their easy access to the drug, doctors and dentists composed approximately 30% of cocaine addicts in the United States at the end of the 19th century. Ironically, many of those doctors had originally used cocaine to overcome their addiction to morphine.

During the early 1900s, cocaine became widely used by all segments of society. Sniffing or "snorting" the drug in powder form became especially popular. Although supposedly only available by prescription, cocaine was sold door to door, in bars, and in brothels. A 1908 article in *The New York Times* under the headline "The Growing Menace of Cocaine" described drugstores as more dangerous than saloons because they sold cocaine and opium. Although black people generally had less money and less access to cocaine than the white population, this drug developed an unfair reputation as a "black" drug, thus fueling even further existing racial prejudice. (In a similar way, racism had motivated much of the criticism of opium use among the Chinese at the end of the 19th century.) Stereotypes aside, white people continued to be the primary abusers of cocaine.

Outlawing Cocaine

The first legislative attempt to stem the tide of cocaine abuse occurred with the passage of the Pure Food and Drug Act in 1906. This law prohibited all interstate shipment of food or soda water containing cocaine. Sensing the change in opinion, the Coca-Cola company had already taken all but a minuscule amount of coca out of its best-selling drink and replaced it with caffeine. By 1912 many states were offering drug edu-

This Aztec art depicts the use of tobacco in two Aztec rituals. Cigarettes originated in Brazil in the mid-1800s.

A 1910 photograph shows three St. Louis newsboys smoking. The annual production of American cigarettes soared from under 18 billion cigarettes in 1915 to 35.3 billion cigarettes two years later.

cation programs to warn students about cocaine and opiates. The Harrison Narcotic Act of 1914 prohibited the use of cocaine in patent medicines and made the recreational use of the drug illegal, as it remains today. Eventually European countries imposed similar narcotics control acts. The Harrison Act remained the basis for federal policy for the next 50 years. As a result, from the 1930s to the late 1960s the abuse of cocaine was largely nonexistent.

Tobacco Addiction Continues Unabated

The last half of the 19th century saw the advent of the cigarette. Cigarettes originated in Brazil, where they were called *papelitos*. By the mid-1800s, they were also being smoked in Spain and France. Soldiers in the Crimean War helped to popularize them, discovering that it was much cheaper to roll their own cigarettes than to buy a ready-made cigar. These early models, however, did not resemble today's cigarettes. For example, the "double cigarette" popular in Austria was almost 12 inches long, had a mouthpiece at each end, and had to be cut in two before it could be smoked.

Although the smoking of cigarettes was becoming increasingly popular during this time, many people still favored cigars. It was all a matter of taste and habit. Napoleon III was an addicted cigarette smoker; Ulysses S. Grant was devoted to cigars. Queen Victoria hated the very idea of smoking and attempted to prohibit the practice in the British army, an especially futile exercise. The great Russian writer Leo Tolstoy was a heavy smoker who tried his best to quit. He could not understand his addiction to a habit he detested. He wrote: "The brain becomes numbed by the nicotine. . . . The stamping out of this fearful disease would mean a new era in the history of mankind." But that era was long distant. By 1913 Americans were smoking 15 billion cigarettes a year, and the cigarette was winning over more and more smokers on both sides of the Atlantic.

Three girls dance the Charleston in a London stage revue. During the Roaring Twenties in Prohibitionist America, the speakeasy (illegal bar) became as much a symbol of the times as was the Charleston.

CHAPTER 6

THE 20TH CENTURY

The 20th century has seen greater use of psychoactive drugs than ever before. Rather than learning from past mistakes regarding their use, people seem to be repeating and magnifying them. International air travel and the ever-growing black market system make every conceivable drug accessible — for a price. As drug use has expanded, there has been an increasing reliance on legislation to bring it under control. But the laws have been flagrantly disregarded. The illegal drug trade has encouraged the rise of organized crime, and large numbers of drug addicts have resorted to criminal acts to secure their "fix."

Prohibition: The Noble Experiment Fails

When Prohibition went into effect in 1920, most of its advocates sincerely believed it would work. One overly confident congressman went so far as to declare: "There is as much chance of repealing the Eighteenth Amendment as there is for a hummingbird to fly to the planet Mars with the Washington Monument tied to its tail." But Prohibition soon spawned a host of problems. Enforcement was extremely difficult, and home production of alcoholic beverages, known as bootlegging, was widespread. Speakeasies, or illegal saloons, seemed to spring up overnight, providing a profitable

Al Capone was the quintessential Chicago bootlegger; his was among the greatest of many fortunes amassed through liquor smuggling during Prohibition. When Capone was finally convicted in 1931, it was not for smuggling but for income tax evasion.

trade for bootleggers. Chicago alone had more than seven thousand illegal drinking establishments. Although Prohibition did indeed reduce per capita consumption of alcohol, it also introduced many Americans to the act of drinking illegal liquor. Just as the use of marijuana became fashionably anti-establishment during the 1960s, unlawful drinking became symbolic of the convention-defying Roaring Twenties. In December 1933 the Eighteenth Amendment was repealed, ending national prohibition and delighting the majority of Americans.

How could the nation's attitude toward drinking change so drastically in 13 years? First, Americans themselves had changed. Much of the original support for prohibition legislation had come from the rural, mainly Protestant section of the country. During the 1920s, however, a powerful new middle class emerged that was composed to a large extent of urban, well-educated Americans, many of whom were recent immigrants and not of the Protestant faith. Members of this class did not generally favor Prohibition. Second, as the Depression began in the 1930s, alcohol sales promised jobs and tax revenue. Finally, the cost of Prohibition was extremely high. The federal government alone had spent $129 million trying to enforce it, and hundreds of lives had been lost in conflict over it. Also, the law had been broken so many times that there was a growing disrespect for laws in general.

No one, however, wanted a return to the excesses of the pre-Prohibition period. Under the new laws, liquor could be purchased only from licensed dealers, and in some states only state-managed stores could sell it. Every state imposed age restrictions — usually a minimum of 18 or 21 years — on those who purchased alcohol. President Franklin Roosevelt even suggested that Americans substitute the more respectable word *tavern* for *saloon*, although the word change did nothing to alter the character of the "new" taverns from their old counterparts.

Alcohol, which is so often a part of adult social gatherings, and nicotine are America's most abused drugs.

The Most Serious Drug Problem

Two years after Prohibition ended, Alcoholics Anonymous (AA), a support group for alcoholics, was born. AA began when Bill Wilson, an alcoholic patient in a New York City hospital, shared his vision of hope with a physician and fellow alcoholic, known as Dr. Bob to preserve his anonymity. Since its founding, AA has emphasized that alcoholism is a disease for which the only cure is total abstinence. Its members are taught that for them "one drink is too many and a thousand are not enough." AA met a need that doctors and psychiatrists could not: it offered friendship and acceptance for alcoholics. Building on a successful reputation, AA has grown to become a worldwide organization with more than 500,000 members.

There are an estimated 10 to 13 million alcoholics (approximately 10% of all drinkers) in the United States, making alcoholism the nation's most serious drug problem. Because alcohol is legal and affordable and has been a part of American culture for so long, it is accepted by people who might shun other psychoactive drugs such as cocaine or marijuana. Also, liquor advertisements invariably depict people who drink as lively, sophisticated, and popular. It is difficult for many Americans, especially young ones, to resist these pressures. In addition, America's liquor stores stock an ever-increasing variety of wine, beer, liqueurs, and hard liquor — a range of choices that people of other ages never imagined.

Marijuana: A New Menace?

During Prohibition a new drug attracted increasing interest in the United States — marijuana. The drug was introduced to the southern part of the nation by Mexican workers as early as 1910. Soon, numerous jazz musicians in New Orleans began to smoke it, as did American sailors stationed in the Panama Canal Zone. Supplies of marijuana also came from Cuba and Central America, traveling up the Mississippi River to the large northern cities. The use of marijuana soon became falsely associated with criminal activities and resulted in growing prejudice against Mexican Americans and blacks. In 1936 a law enforcement official in New Orleans claimed that 60% of the crimes in that city were associated with marijuana.

Aroused in part by exaggerated statistics, 16 states had prohibited the use of marijuana by 1930. The Federal Bureau of Narcotics campaigned against the "killer drug," describing the marijuana user as a "fiend with savage or caveman tendencies." Although the American Medical Association denied that marijuana caused violent behavior, a surge of antimarijuana sentiment brought about the federal Marijuana Tax Act in 1937. The act levied a $100 tax per ounce on all unregistered use of the drug. The law did not directly prohibit the use of marijuana but made it so expensive that trading in the drug became part of the underworld drug market.

Those who did not consider marijuana a "menace" were a vocal minority. In 1942 the *American Journal of Psychiatry* suggested that marijuana was not as habit-forming as alcohol or tobacco. Shortly thereafter, a team of New York scientists undertook a careful examination of the drug. In 1944 they published the "LaGuardia Report," which concluded that although marijuana lowered inhibitions it did not lead to aggressive behavior. Major medical journals were split in their

Jazz players performing in New Orleans during the 1920s. The popularity of marijuana among black musicians, which began during Prohibition, led many legislators unjustly to stereotype blacks as drug abusers and street criminals.

Timothy Leary, a former Harvard psychology professor, discusses LSD. His advice to "turn on, tune in, and drop out" in 1967 was the cue for thousands of college students to experiment with psychedelic drugs.

reaction to the report. The *Journal of the American Medical Association* called the report "narrow and thoroughly unscientific." On the other hand, *Science* magazine called it a "substantial contribution" having "considerable value."

After World War II the Federal Bureau of Narcotics continued its campaign against marijuana use. For most of the nation, marijuana was still a relatively unfamiliar drug. People who attended lectures sponsored by the Narcotics Bureau or who saw the frightening government film *Marijuana* became alarmed. The misinformation spread by the Bureau did much to damage the credibility of more responsible drug education programs that followed.

In the 1960s marijuana use became more popular than ever before. Many college students, rock musicians, and antiwar activists advocated smoking marijuana not only for its intoxicating effects but as an act of rebellion against parental and governmental authority. Marijuana use began to decline in the 1970s because of increasing knowledge of the drug's potential negative effects on such things as memory retention, social interaction, motor coordination, concentration, and grasp of reality itself.

LSD: The Synthetic Hallucinogen

Another drug widely used in the 1960s was lysergic acid diethylamide or LSD, a very potent hallucinogen. The history of drugs is full of accidental discoveries, but LSD's discovery was an accident suited to the modern age — it occurred in a chemistry laboratory. In 1943 the German chemist Albert Hofmann was attempting to purify lysergic acid when a trace of the substance was absorbed through his skin. Suddenly he felt dizzy and restless. He experienced, in his words, "fantastic pictures, extraordinary shapes with intense, kaleidoscopic

Betty Ford, the former first lady, recovered from dependency on pills and alcohol and discussed her problems frankly and publicly. After her recovery, she opened the Betty Ford Center for Chemical Dependency, a rehabilitation center in California.

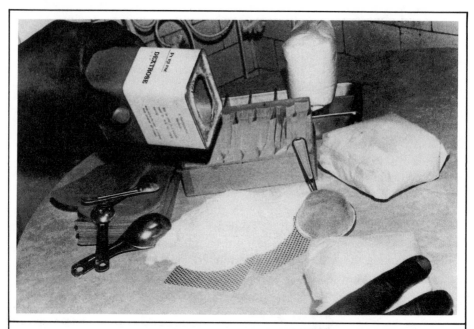

Heroin is cut with dextrose in a New York "factory." The drug is so expensive that many addicts turn to crime to maintain their habit.

play of colors." A few days later he experimented by drinking a very small amount of the drug. The terrifying visions and profound physical discomfort that followed convinced him that he had stumbled upon an unusually powerful hallucinogen. He wrote: "This drug makes normal people psychotic."

LSD soon attracted the interest of psychiatrists, whose experiments with the drug in turn attracted writers, artists, and then the general public. Many people were enthusiastic about their LSD "trips" and insisted that the hallucinogen gave them a clearer view of reality. In actuality the opposite was true. Soon LSD began to be manufactured illegally, and dosages became highly unreliable. Terrifying trips scared off many users, and some people suffered lasting psychological damage. By the 1980s the use of LSD had subsided somewhat, in part because of controversial publicity about its ability to cause chromosome damage. A few psychiatrists continue to use the drug in controlled settings as a treatment for severe forms of mental illness, such as schizophrenia.

Driving Heroin Addiction Underground

Another widely abused drug is heroin, the substance most people associate with the term *drug addict* and with crime. In fact, the typical drug addict is more likely to be an alcoholic (there are approximately half a million heroin addicts in the United States and 10 to 13 million alcoholics). Because heroin is illegal and expensive, addicts often resort to crime to maintain their habit, and heroin addicts form a kind of criminal subculture in most large American cities. But this has not always been the case.

First produced in Germany in 1898, heroin derived its name, ironically, for its supposedly "heroic" power to cure morphine addiction. When the Harrison Act of 1914 outlawed over-the-counter narcotic drugs, addicts became dependent on physicians for their supply. But since opiate addiction was considered a moral problem rather than a disease at that time, doctors were increasingly ostracized for dispensing drugs to their addict patients. Many physicians served prison sentences for prescribing illegal drugs. Clinics sprang up to rehabilitate or maintain addicts, but misguided public opposition to such facilities forced most of them to close down. Addicts went underground and became the prey of organized crime. Thus, by attempting to reduce the existing drug problem, the Harrison Act in effect created an entirely new one.

Today there are approximately one-half million heroin addicts in the United States. The 1980s have witnessed not only a prospering multibillion-dollar international market in narcotics, but also a striking change in the profile of the average heroin user, as many wealthy, educated, and white-collar professionals have succumbed to the addictive properties of a drug that generally has been associated with the urban poor.

Abuse of Prescription Drugs

In the 1950s and 1960s many people — especially women — began using barbiturates for their anxiety-reducing and sleep-inducing properties. Drug companies developed a new class of drugs called minor tranquilizers, of which Valium (brand name for diazepam) and Librium (brand name for chlordiazepoxide) were the most widely used. Other sedative-hypnotics (drugs that produce calmness, relaxation, and, at high doses, sleep), such as the sleeping pill methaqualone (commonly known as Quaalude), became increasingly popular.

In a highly competitive industry, drug companies often brought out these new products without having done sufficient research. For example, Librium was promoted as a cure for alcoholism; instead it frequently caused dual addiction. Because Valium initially appeared to be relatively harmless and nonaddicting, many thousands of doctors prescribed it to relieve stress or insomnia. Darvon, a narcotic that was introduced as a relatively safe painkiller in 1957, was the leading cause of death among legal drugs in 1977, claiming 320 lives. In addition, barbiturates and tranquilizers soon became highly abused "recreational drugs," available on the underground market.

Who was to blame for America's infatuation with "pill-popping?" The drug companies, in part, which gained enormous profit. The medical community, in part, whose pres-

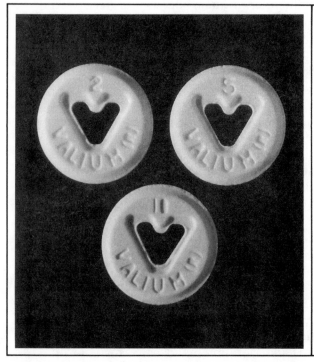

Valium, introduced in 1963, quickly became the most widely prescribed tranquilizer. But when doctors and prominent public figures began to speak out about the dangers of prescription-drug dependency and abuse, tranquilizer sales declined.

tigious journals are largely financed by drug advertisements. Doctors were to blame for relying on drugs as the easiest, fastest way to help their patients. The patients themselves were to blame for being too trusting, for not asking questions about their medications, and for seeking painless ways to avoid their problems. Finally, some people blamed modern society itself, with its social and work-related stress, economic uncertainty, the threat of nuclear war, loss of strong religious faith and spiritual values, and demands for instant gratification.

By the mid-1970s, however, physicians had become sadly aware of the addictive and lethal potential of these drugs. The combination of alcohol and barbiturates is especially toxic, since each is a central-nervous-system depressant that enhances the other's effects. Because of increasing evidence concerning the potential hazards of these drugs, physicians became more conservative about prescribing them. Prominent figures like former First Lady Betty Ford, who suffered addiction to both barbiturates and alcohol, helped publicize their dangers. Valium sales declined by 50% between 1975 and 1980; its use and the use of other sedatives continue to decrease. The use of Quaaludes has been illegal since 1982.

Unfortunately, as the use of tranquilizers and barbiturates subsided in the late 1970s, cocaine use increased. A growing number of people argued, foolishly and dangerously, that cocaine had been falsely maligned and had been rejected largely because of racial prejudice. In the 1980s cocaine has attracted a younger, wealthier clientele, and its use has become pervasive throughout all segments of society. Crack, an intensely addictive, less expensive form of cocaine, has become widely available in large cities, and in 1986 its abuse reached epidemic proportions.

Tobacco Use on the Wane

While the use of most drugs increased in the 20th century, tobacco smoking in the United States finally began to decrease. As early as 1928 major medical journals began to report more cancer, more heart disease, and a reduced life expectancy among smokers than among nonsmokers. A number of doctors cautioned against smoking, but their warnings

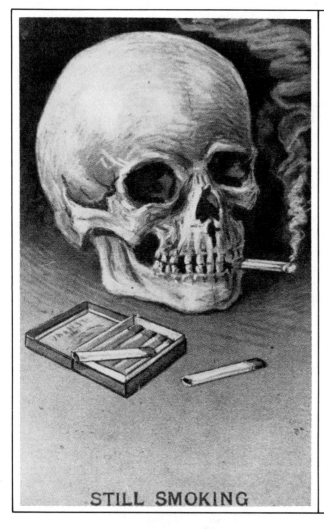

STILL SMOKING

A 1910 poster warns of the dangers of smoking. The anti-tobacco movement has gained momentum throughout this century; two examples of its effectiveness are the ban on all television advertising of cigarettes and mounting opposition to smoking in public places.

were largely unheeded. Between 1920 and 1930 the consumption of cigarettes doubled. Cigarettes were in such demand during World War II that draft boards offered deferments to tobacco farmers. Even the American Medical Association went along with popular opinion. In fact, until 1981 the AMA owned more than $1 million worth of stock in the nation's two largest tobacco companies.

Armed with increasing evidence, many prominent doctors in the 1950s formed an antismoking crusade, including in their ranks the U.S. Surgeon General. In 1960 the American

Cancer Society concluded "beyond reasonable doubt" that cigarette smoking caused lung cancer. The American public was still heavily influenced by the tobacco industry, an $82-billion-a-year enterprise, the power of whose advertising cannot be overstated.

In 1964 a presidential commission released a report concluding that cigarette smoking was a primary cause of lung cancer, emphysema, chronic bronchitis, and heart disease. Finally, the message about the dangers of tobacco began to hit home. Cigarette sales dropped 20% in the seven weeks following that report. Cigarette smokers in the United States have fallen from 42% of the adult population in 1965 to 30% in 1986.

Today, cigarette packages must carry warnings stating that cigarette smoking is a health hazard. Airlines and many restaurants have nonsmoking sections. In 1986 the Pentagon mounted an aggressive campaign against smoking in the armed forces, traditionally a bastion of heavy smokers. That same year the American Cancer Society changed the focus of its "War Against Cancer" from cure to prevention, a goal that will entail stronger efforts to educate people about the dangers of smoking. But these changes have taken place only in the United States. Tobacco consumption in the rest of the world has increased by 75% over the past 20 years.

YOU CAN REALLY GO PLACES WITH CRACK.

CHAPTER 7

FUTURE AGES

Psychoactive drugs have been a part of every historical age and probably always will be. The best hope for the future lies in understanding and emphasizing drug controls that have worked in the past and are still working today.

Religious Value Systems

Religion is the oldest of these controls. This is somewhat ironic, since a particular drug is sometimes the centerpiece for the most sacred part of a religious ritual. For example, alcoholism is virtually nonexistent among Orthodox Jews because alcohol in the form of wine is so closely associated with many aspects of Jewish worship. From infancy, Orthodox Jews learn that wine is a ritualistic drink used to observe many occasions, but never for becoming drunk.

Religions have also taken moral positions against certain drugs. Religion offers spiritual beliefs that help people cope with life's problems without resorting to drugs. Churches also provide the sense of community so frequently missing in contemporary society. It is somehow fitting that Alcoholics Anonymous meetings are often held in churches, since part of AA's success can be attributed to the group's heavy emphasis on spiritual values. In the future, religion will probably continue to be an important control over drug use, especially if churches focus on drug education and counseling.

The American Cancer Society, which produced this anti-smoking poster, educates people of all ages about the dangers of tobacco, and also runs prevention and withdrawal programs.

Medical Science

Medicine is another ancient control that continues to be effective. The decline in cigarette smoking is an obvious example of the positive influence of medical knowledge on the use of a psychoactive drug. Future ages may wonder why people ever took delight in filling their lungs with carbon monoxide, nicotine, and other poisons. Similarly, scientific evidence of serious health risks helped reduce abuse of tranquilizers and barbiturates, LSD, and marijuana in the 1970s. Enough questions have been raised about caffeine to turn many consumers to decaffeinated coffee. Research will probably provide new evidence of hazards lurking in other drugs.

Legislation

The courts have continued to pass legislation calling for stiffer penalties for convicted drug sellers and abusers in an effort to put the reins on drug trafficking. For example, lawmakers have intensified their battle against organized crime, especially in America's urban centers and port cities, through which drugs enter the country in great quantities. In addition, cooperation between the governments of the many nations concerned with the global problem of drug abuse has created avenues by which the authorities can effectively wage war on the international drug market. In spite of these efforts, profits from drug selling continue to be astronomical, and drug abuse remains a major concern for legislators. Still, in many ways the legislative assault on drug abuse in America has only just started; the war will continue to escalate.

Drug Education

Education has the greatest potential for controlling drug use. The power of education is illustrated by the behavior of young people, who have been better educated than older generations regarding the dangers of cigarette smoking. College-bound high school seniors are more than two times less likely to smoke than are seniors who do not plan to go to college. If drug education programs are honest and are careful not to exaggerate their warnings about the dangers of abuse, they can be effective. Better education for doctors is also essential in the future. Too often physicians have casually prescribed drugs as the easiest way to fulfill their patients' immediate needs.

In the future, scientists will undoubtedly discover new psychoactive drugs and invent synthetic ones. How will the human race respond to these new substances? Will they be promoted as less addictive, safer drugs? Will they offer a "cure" for other addictions? Whatever the claims, if people are familiar with the history of drugs and remember the mistakes of the past, they will be able to make more intelligent decisions about using drugs in the years to come.

APPENDIX

State Agencies
for the Prevention and Treatment
of Drug Abuse

ALABAMA
Department of Mental Health
Division of Mental Illness and
  Substance Abuse Community
  Programs
200 Interstate Park Drive
P.O. Box 3710
Montgomery, AL 36193
(205) 271-9253

ALASKA
Department of Health and Social
  Services
Office of Alcoholism and Drug
  Abuse
Pouch H-05-F
Juneau, AK 99811
(907) 586-6201

ARIZONA
Department of Health Services
Division of Behavioral Health
  Services
Bureau of Community Services
Alcohol Abuse and Alcoholism
  Section
2500 East Van Buren
Phoenix, AZ 85008
(602) 255-1238

Department of Health Services
Division of Behavioral Health
  Services
Bureau of Community Services
Drug Abuse Section
2500 East Van Buren
Phoenix, AZ 85008
(602) 255-1240

ARKANSAS
Department of Human Services
Office on Alcohol and Drug Abuse
  Prevention
1515 West 7th Avenue
Suite 310
Little Rock, AR 72202
(501) 371-2603

CALIFORNIA
Department of Alcohol and Drug
  Abuse
111 Capitol Mall
Sacramento, CA 95814
(916) 445-1940

COLORADO
Department of Health
Alcohol and Drug Abuse Division
4210 East 11th Avenue
Denver, CO 80220
(303) 320-6137

CONNECTICUT
Alcohol and Drug Abuse
  Commission
999 Asylum Avenue
3rd Floor
Hartford, CT 06105
(203) 566-4145

DELAWARE
Division of Mental Health
Bureau of Alcoholism and Drug
  Abuse
1901 North Dupont Highway
Newcastle, DE 19720
(302) 421-6101

DISTRICT OF COLUMBIA
Department of Human Services
Office of Health Planning and
  Development
601 Indiana Avenue, NW
Suite 500
Washington, D.C. 20004
(202) 724-5641

FLORIDA
Department of Health and
  Rehabilitative Services
Alcoholic Rehabilitation Program
1317 Winewood Boulevard
Room 187A
Tallahassee, FL 32301
(904) 488-0396

Department of Health and
  Rehabilitative Services
Drug Abuse Program
1317 Winewood Boulevard
Building 6, Room 155
Tallahassee, FL 32301
(904) 488-0900

GEORGIA
Department of Human Resources
Division of Mental Health and
  Mental Retardation
Alcohol and Drug Section
618 Ponce De Leon Avenue, NE
Atlanta, GA 30365-2101
(404) 894-4785

HAWAII
Department of Health
Mental Health Division
Alcohol and Drug Abuse Branch
1250 Punch Bowl Street
P.O. Box 3378
Honolulu, HI 96801
(808) 548-4280

IDAHO
Department of Health and Welfare
Bureau of Preventive Medicine
Substance Abuse Section
450 West State
Boise, ID 83720
(208) 334-4368

ILLINOIS
Department of Mental Health and
  Developmental Disabilities
Division of Alcoholism
160 North La Salle Street
Room 1500
Chicago, IL 60601
(312) 793-2907

Illinois Dangerous Drugs
  Commission
300 North State Street
Suite 1500
Chicago, IL 60610
(312) 822-9860

INDIANA
Department of Mental Health
Division of Addiction Services
429 North Pennsylvania Street
Indianapolis, IN 46204
(317) 232-7816

IOWA
Department of Substance Abuse
505 5th Avenue
Insurance Exchange Building
Suite 202
Des Moines, IA 50319
(515) 281-3641

KANSAS
Department of Social Rehabilitation
Alcohol and Drug Abuse Services
2700 West 6th Street
Biddle Building
Topeka, KS 66606
(913) 296-3925

KENTUCKY
Cabinet for Human Resources
Department of Health Services
Substance Abuse Branch
275 East Main Street
Frankfort, KY 40601
(502) 564-2880

LOUISIANA
Department of Health and Human
  Resources
Office of Mental Health and
  Substance Abuse
655 North 5th Street
P.O. Box 4049
Baton Rouge, LA 70821
(504) 342-2565

MAINE
Department of Human Services
Office of Alcoholism and Drug
  Abuse Prevention
Bureau of Rehabilitation
32 Winthrop Street
Augusta, ME 04330
(207) 289-2781

MARYLAND
Alcoholism Control Administration
201 West Preston Street
Fourth Floor
Baltimore, MD 21201
(301) 383-2977

State Health Department
Drug Abuse Administration
201 West Preston Street
Baltimore, MD 21201
(301) 383-3312

MASSACHUSETTS
Department of Public Health
Division of Alcoholism
755 Boylston Street
Sixth Floor
Boston, MA 02116
(617) 727-1960

Department of Public Health
Division of Drug Rehabilitation
600 Washington Street
Boston, MA 02114
(617) 727-8617

MICHIGAN
Department of Public Health
Office of Substance Abuse Services
3500 North Logan Street
P.O. Box 30035
Lansing, MI 48909
(517) 373-8603

MINNESOTA
Department of Public Welfare
Chemical Dependency Program
  Division
Centennial Building
658 Cedar Street
4th Floor
Saint Paul, MN 55155
(612) 296-4614

MISSISSIPPI
Department of Mental Health
Division of Alcohol and Drug Abuse
1102 Robert E. Lee Building
Jackson, MS 39201
(601) 359-1297

MISSOURI
Department of Mental Health
Division of Alcoholism and Drug
  Abuse
2002 Missouri Boulevard
P.O. Box 687
Jefferson City, MO 65102
(314) 751-4942

MONTANA
Department of Institutions
Alcohol and Drug Abuse Division
1539 11th Avenue
Helena, MT 59620
(406) 449-2827

94

NEBRASKA
Department of Public Institutions
Division of Alcoholism and Drug Abuse
801 West Van Dorn Street
P.O. Box 94728
Lincoln, NB 68509
(402) 471-2851, Ext. 415

NEVADA
Department of Human Resources
Bureau of Alcohol and Drug Abuse
505 East King Street
Carson City, NV 89710
(702) 885-4790

NEW HAMPSHIRE
Department of Health and Welfare
Office of Alcohol and Drug Abuse
   Prevention
Hazen Drive
Health and Welfare Building
Concord, NH 03301
(603) 271-4627

NEW JERSEY
Department of Health
Division of Alcoholism
129 East Hanover Street CN 362
Trenton, NJ 08625
(609) 292-8949

Department of Health
Division of Narcotic and Drug Abuse
   Control
129 East Hanover Street CN 362
Trenton, NJ 08625
(609) 292-8949

NEW MEXICO
Health and Environment Department
Behavioral Services Division
Substance Abuse Bureau
725 Saint Michaels Drive
P.O. Box 968
Santa Fe, NM 87503
(505) 984-0020, Ext. 304

NEW YORK
Division of Alcoholism and Alcohol
   Abuse
194 Washington Avenue
Albany, NY 12210
(518) 474-5417

Division of Substance Abuse
   Services
Executive Park South
Box 8200
Albany, NY 12203
(518) 457-7629

NORTH CAROLINA
Department of Human Resources
Division of Mental Health, Mental
   Retardation and Substance Abuse
   Services
Alcohol and Drug Abuse Services
325 North Salisbury Street
Albemarle Building
Raleigh, NC 27611
(919) 733-4670

NORTH DAKOTA
Department of Human Services
Division of Alcoholism and Drug
   Abuse
State Capitol Building
Bismarck, ND 58505
(701) 224-2767

OHIO
Department of Health
Division of Alcoholism
246 North High Street
P.O. Box 118
Columbus, OH 43216
(614) 466-3543

Department of Mental Health
Bureau of Drug Abuse
65 South Front Street
Columbus, OH 43215
(614) 466-9023

OKLAHOMA
Department of Mental Health
Alcohol and Drug Programs
4545 North Lincoln Boulevard
Suite 100 East Terrace
P.O. Box 53277
Oklahoma City, OK 73152
(405) 521-0044

OREGON
Department of Human Resources
Mental Health Division
Office of Programs for Alcohol and
Drug Problems
2575 Bittern Street, NE
Salem, OR 97310
(503) 378-2163

PENNSYLVANIA
Department of Health
Office of Drug and Alcohol
Programs
Commonwealth and Forster Avenues
Health and Welfare Building
P.O. Box 90
Harrisburg, PA 17108
(717) 787-9857

RHODE ISLAND
Department of Mental Health,
Mental Retardation and Hospitals
Division of Substance Abuse
Substance Abuse Administration
Building
Cranston, RI 02920
(401) 464-2091

SOUTH CAROLINA
Commission on Alcohol and Drug
Abuse
3700 Forest Drive
Columbia, SC 29204
(803) 758-2521

SOUTH DAKOTA
Department of Health
Division of Alcohol and Drug Abuse
523 East Capitol, Joe Foss Building
Pierre, SD 57501
(605) 773-4806

TENNESSEE
Department of Mental Health and
Mental Retardation
Alcohol and Drug Abuse Services
505 Deaderick Street
James K. Polk Building, Fourth Floor
Nashville, TN 37219
(615) 741-1921

TEXAS
Commission on Alcoholism
809 Sam Houston State Office Building
Austin, TX 78701
(512) 475-2577

Department of Community Affairs
Drug Abuse Prevention Division
2015 South Interstate Highway 35
P.O. Box 13166
Austin, TX 78711
(512) 443-4100

UTAH
Department of Social Services
Division of Alcoholism and Drugs
150 West North Temple
Suite 350
P.O. Box 2500
Salt Lake City, UT 84110
(801) 533-6532

VERMONT
Agency of Human Services
Department of Social and
Rehabilitation Services
Alcohol and Drug Abuse Division
103 South Main Street
Waterbury, VT 05676
(802) 241-2170

VIRGINIA
Department of Mental Health and
 Mental Retardation
Division of Substance Abuse
109 Governor Street
P.O. Box 1797
Richmond, VA 23214
(804) 786-5313

WASHINGTON
Department of Social and Health
 Service
Bureau of Alcohol and Substance
 Abuse
Office Building—44 W
Olympia, WA 98504
(206) 753-5866

WEST VIRGINIA
Department of Health
Office of Behavioral Health Services
Division on Alcoholism and Drug
 Abuse
1800 Washington Street East
Building 3 Room 451
Charleston, WV 25305
(304) 348-2276

WISCONSIN
Department of Health and Social
 Services
Division of Community Services
Bureau of Community Programs
Alcohol and Other Drug Abuse
 Program Office
1 West Wilson Street
P.O. Box 7851
Madison, WI 53707
(608) 266-2717

WYOMING
Alcohol and Drug Abuse Programs
Hathaway Building
Cheyenne, WY 82002
(307) 777-7115, Ext. 7118

GUAM
Mental Health & Substance Abuse
 Agency
P.O. Box 20999
Guam 96921

PUERTO RICO
Department of Addiction Control
 Services
Alcohol Abuse Programs
P.O. Box B-Y Rio Piedras Station
Rio Piedras, PR 00928
(809) 763-5014

Department of Addiction Control
 Services
Drug Abuse Programs
P.O. Box B-Y Rio Piedras Station
Rio Piedras, PR 00928
(809) 764-8140

VIRGIN ISLANDS
Division of Mental Health,
 Alcoholism & Drug Dependency
 Services
P.O. Box 7329
Saint Thomas, Virgin Islands 00801
(809) 774-7265

AMERICAN SAMOA
LBJ Tropical Medical Center
Department of Mental Health Clinic
Pago Pago, American Samoa 96799

TRUST TERRITORIES
Director of Health Services
Office of the High Commissioner
Saipan, Trust Territories 96950

Further Reading

Anderson, Frank J. *An Illustrated History of the Herbals*. New York: Columbia University Press, 1977.

Chafetz, Morris E. *Liquor: The Servant of Man*. Boston: Little, Brown and Company, 1965.

Coffey, Thomas M. *The Long Thirst: Prohibition in America: 1920–1933*. New York: Dell Publishing Company, 1975.

Freud, Sigmund. *Cocaine Papers*. Robert Byck, ed. New York: New American Library, 1975.

Goode, Erich. *Drugs in American Society*. Second Edition. New York: Alfred A. Knopf, 1984.

Grinspoon, Lester and Bakalar, James B. *Cocaine: A Drug and Its Social Evolution*. New York: Basic Books, Inc., 1976.

Kaplan, John. *Marijuana — The New Prohibition*. New York: The World Publishing Company, 1970.

Schultes, Richard Evans and Hofmann, Albert. *Plants of the Gods; Origins of Hallucinogenic Use*. New York: McGraw-Hill Book Company, 1979.

Weil, Andrew and Rosen, Winifred. *Chocolate to Morphine: Understanding Mind-Active Drugs*. Boston: Houghton Mifflin Company, 1983.

Glossary

abstinence: voluntary refrainment from the use of alcohol and/or other drugs

addiction: a condition caused by repeated drug use, characterized by a compulsive urge to continue using the drug, a tendency to increase the dosage, and physiological and/or psychological dependence

anesthetic: a drug that produces loss of sensation, sometimes without loss of consciousness

barbiturate: a drug that causes depression of the central nervous system, generally used to reduce anxiety or to induce euphoria

caffeine: trimethylxanthine; a central nervous system stimulant found in coffee, tea, cocoa, and various soft drinks

cocaine: the primary psychoactive ingredient in the coca plant; it functions as a behavioral stimulant

crack: a chemically modified, less expensive, highly addictive form of cocaine

ether: an organic compound composed of oxygen, carbon, and hydrogen, such as diethyl ether ($C_4H_{10}O$), the form used to produce anesthesia

euphoria: a mental high characterized by a sense of well-being

fly agaric: a brightly colored mushroom; causes hallucinations and delirium, sometimes alternating with convulsions or depressive trances

genus: a category of related plants; part of a system of classification developed by the Swedish physician Carolus Linnaeus

hallucinogen: a drug that produces sensory impressions that have no basis in reality

heroin: a semisynthetic opiate produced by a chemical modification of morphine

LSD: lysergic acid diethylamide; a hallucinogen derived from a fungus that grows on rye or from morning-glory seeds

marijuana: the leaves, flowers, buds, and/or branches of the hemp plant, *Cannabis sativa* or *Cannabis indica*, that contain cannabinoids, a group of intoxicating drugs

morphine: the principal psychoactive ingredient in opium; it is used for its pain-relieving and sedative properties

narcotic: originally, a group of drugs producing effects similar to morphine; often used to refer to any substance that sedates, has a depressive effect, and/or causes dependence

opiate: any compound from the milky juice of the poppy plant, including opium, morphine, codeine, and their derivatives, such as heroin

organic: derived from a living organism and containing carbon and hydrogen

peyote: a cactus that contains mescaline, a hallucinogenic drug; it is used legally by certain American Indians for religious and medical purposes

physical dependence: an adaptation of the body to the presence of a drug such that its absence produces withdrawal symptoms

psychoactive: altering mood and/or behavior

psychological dependence: a condition in which the drug user craves a drug to maintain a sense of well-being and feels discomfort when deprived of it

sedative: a drug that produces calmness, relaxation, and, at high doses, sleep

shaman: a medicine man or woman; shamans often preside over ceremonies involving hallucinogens in Mexico and other Latin American countries

snuff: a substance made from powdered tobacco and inhaled through the nose; snuff was extremely popular in France in the seventeenth century during the reign of Louis XIV

tolerance: an adaptation of the cells of the body to the effects of a drug, such that the drug user requires higher doses of the drug to achieve the effects he or she experienced previously

tranquilizer: a drug that has calming, relaxing effects; includes Valium

withdrawal: the physiological and psychological effects that occur after the use of a drug is discontinued

Picture Credits

American Cancer Society: p. 90; AP/Wide World Photos: pp. 10, 80, 81, 82; Art Resource: pp. 24, 27, 32, 42, 54, 77; The Bettmann Archive: pp. 8, 20, 36, 37, 38, 43, 45, 46, 47, 48, 49, 52, 57, 58, 60, 62, 65, 66, 67, 69, 74, 76, 79, 86; Peter T. Furst: p. 30; Hoffman LaRoche Laboratories: p. 84; The Metropolitan Museum of Art: pp. 12, 22, 25, 40, 72; New York Public Library Picture Collection: pp. 35, 56, 71; Newsday: p. 88; Scala/Art Resource: pp. 18, 28, 50, 51, 64.

Index

Jean McBee Knox is a writer who specializes in medicine and social issues. Her articles have appeared in the *Boston Globe,* the *Globe Sunday Magazine,* the *Christian Science Monitor,* and other publications. A graduate of Wheaton College and Wesleyan University, she has taught English in Greenwich, Connecticut and Winchester, Massachusetts.

Solomon H. Snyder, M.D. is Distinguished Service Professor of Neuroscience, Pharmacology and Psychiatry at The Johns Hopkins University School of Medicine. He has served as president of the Society for Neuroscience and in 1978 received the Albert Lasker Award in Medical Research. He has authored *Uses of Marijuana, Madness and the Brain, The Troubled Mind, Biological Aspects of Mental Disorder,* and edited *Perspective in Neuropharmacology: A Tribute to Julius Axelrod.* Professor Snyder was a research associate with Dr. Axelrod at the National Institutes of Health.

Barry L. Jacobs, Ph.D., is currently a professor in the program of neuroscience at Princeton University. Professor Jacobs is author of *Serotonin Neurotransmission and Behavior* and *Hallucinogens: Neurochemical, Behavioral and Clinical Perspectives.* He has written many journal articles in the field of neuroscience and contributed numerous chapters to books on behavior and brain science. He has been a member of several panels of the National Institute of Mental Health.

Joann Ellison Rodgers, M.S. (Columbia), became Deputy Director of Public Affairs and Director of Media Relations for the Johns Hopkins Medical Institutions in Baltimore, Maryland, in 1984 after 18 years as an award-winning science journalist and widely read columnist for the Hearst newspapers.